Southern California's Best
Ghost Towns

DAT

The Eastern California Museum's outdoor display, with the Sierra Nevadas in the background

Southern California's Best Ghost Towns

A Practical Guide

By Philip Varney

Photographs by the Author

Maps and Drawings by James M. Davis

University of Oklahoma Press : NORMAN AND LONDON

By Philip Varney

Arizona's Best Ghost Towns: A Practical Guide (Flagstaff, 1980)
New Mexico's Best Ghost Towns: A Practical Guide (Albuquerque, 1987)
Southern California's Best Ghost Towns (Norman, 1990)

Maps by James M. Davis

Library of Congress Cataloging-in-Publication Data

Varney, Philip.
    Southern California's best ghost towns : a practical guide / by
Philip Varney : photographs by the author ; maps and drawings by
James M. Davis.—1st ed.
        p.   cm.
    Includes bibliographical references.
    ISBN 0-8061-2252-8 (alk. paper)
    1. Cities and towns, Ruined, extinct, etc.—California, Southern—
Guide-books.   2. California, Southern—Description and travel—
Guide-books.   I. Title.
F867.V34   1990
917.94′9—dc20   89-22742
                                                                    CIP

For Mary Ann Mead

Contents

Acknowledgments

I wish to express my appreciation:

To Freeman Hover, Bill Broyles, Jim Price, and Ned and Margaret Marshall—good friends who know what I do and who are constantly on the lookout for books, articles, and rumors that concern life on the back roads.

To Mike Davis, for exceptional drawings and maps.

To Alan Hensher, for opening his files and supplying valuable information on Mojave Desert ghost towns.

To Bill Drum, Dave McDonald, Don Leach, Dale Mann, Sue Krieg, and Louann Frino, for instruction and assistance with word processing.

To Chris Ziegler and Dale Steele, for their tireless help in the Map Collections of the University of Arizona Library.

To Myles and Erna Veltman, who gave me a royal tour of Cerro Gordo on my first visit and would accept nothing but thanks.

To Larry Charpied, for driving me all around Eagle Mountain.

To Barry Menges (Mitchell Caverns), Ross Hopkins, Shirley Harding, and Bill Schreier (Death Valley), for giving me the inside information about their backyards.

To Jack and Linda Laughlin, who gave us an up-hill lift to Panamint so we could have the mountain bike downhill of a lifetime.

To Oscar Gonzales, John Hoge, and Adalberto Aguilar, for recounting the story of Cargo Muchacho.

To Kaiser Steel Corporation and Phelps Dodge Corporation for their efforts in protecting and preserving mining sites and buildings.

To trip companions Warren Weaver, George Jacoby, Jim Holland, Jim Price, and Joan Sieber, who served as navigators, notetakers, counselors, and friends.

To my mother, Betty Varney, who typed my first two books and who would gladly have typed this one had she not been retired by the genie in the computer.

To my daughter Janet, who has had to surrender her father to California and the library on numerous occasions, but has done so without complaint.

To three people who gave me encouragement and love but are no longer here to read the result—lifelong friends Laura Durgin and Mike Psaltis, and my father, F. C. Varney.

And most of all, to Mary Ann Mead—to whom this book is dedicated—who worked next to me in the map rooms, rode the back roads by truck and by bicycle, proofed the text, and prodded me when I needed it.

PHILIP VARNEY

Tucson

To the Reader

I am a dedicated back-roads traveler. After a decade of searching for ghost towns, in 1980 I published *Arizona's Best Ghost Towns* as a result of some frustration with the way ghost town books were put together; I wanted a totally practical, informative guide that would contain all the details I had needed next to me on the seat of my truck. My first book's success encouraged me to write *New Mexico's Best Ghost Towns,* which followed the format of the first.

I then turned my attention to the west. I was surprised, but delighted, to discover that although California has several ghost town books, no one book surveyed the entire state the way I thought it should be covered. So I began, in the summer of 1981, a project I felt certain would take several years of work, thousands of miles of driving, and summers and vacations of solid delight. What became apparent as the fieldwork continued was that I was actually writing two books. The scope of the project would result in one book too ponderous and too expensive to be placed where it belongs—on the seat of your vehicle as you head toward the rewarding adventure that is ghost towning.

So, one-half of the original project is in your hands. First, a word about the title of this book—*Southern California's Best Ghost Towns.* I know that Chapters One and Two are areas that many Californians would not consider Southern California; however, it seemed appropriate to expand the area to include Inyo and Kern counties. My alternative was to call this book *California's Best Ghost Towns,* Volume Two. Volume One, after all, would be the book containing the sites that began the stampede to California—the Gold Rush of 1849. But that book, while it is in the works, would not be finished before this one. So, I took the risk of arousing the wrath of good people living in places like Independence and Lake Isabella and included them in a Southern California volume. I think there is justification for such an inclusion anyway. After all, the major connections of the Death Valley, Inyo, and Kern county mines for food, supplies, shipping of ore, and, often, financial backing were with Los Angeles, not San Francisco—the attachment was to the south, not the north. My Northern book, incidentally, is being written using the same format as this one and will include sites from the Gold Rush Country, the Eastern Sierra, the Bay Area, and on up to the Oregon border.

So, what are the essential questions that I believe ghost town enthusiasts really need to know in order to plan excursions and make on-site explorations? They include the following:

- Do I need more than a road map, and if so, which map or maps do I need?
- What is actually there at the site, *now,* in the way of buildings, mines, or ruins?
- Is the site open to the public?
- Which are the sites I really *must* see and which ones can I pass up if I don't have time to see them all?
- What are the normal road conditions of the route?
- How much can I reasonably expect to see in a given period of time?

To answer those questions, each chapter provides the reader with:

- a map of the area drawn to emphasize the towns and essential back roads
- individual entries containing current photographs, directions, history, and special points of interest
- a capsule summary of the sites in the chapter, ranking them in order as either "major," "secondary," or "minor" spots
- road conditions, indicating the type of vehicle recommended
- trip suggestions, including approximate time allotments and mileage
- a topographic map information chart, providing names of area maps and the degree to which each is essential for finding and exploring sites

Every single site in this book was visited at least once in the 1980s, most between 1984 and 1988. Time will, unfortunately, make some of the photographs obsolete, but I have tried to emphasize major buildings and ruins, attractions that one can only hope will endure.

Appendixes at the end of the book give information that the seasoned back-roads explorer may not utilize often but others may find essential.

- Appendix A will help you learn how to read and use topographic maps effectively.
- Appendix B gives a primer on the most frequently used mining terms.
- Appendix C, a pronunciation guide, can save you the embarrassment of mispronouncing someone's hometown.
- Appendix D enumerates basic suggestions for traveling the backroads safely.
- Appendix E tells of an excellent way to visit ghost towns—by bicycle.
- Appendix F lists sites, mentioned in other ghost

town books, that I visited but have chosen not to include.

Here are some fundamentals for enjoyable ghost towning:

- Read the appropriate chapter and study maps before you go.
- Let someone know precisely where you're going and when you plan to return.
- Secure permission to visit sites when necessary. Often a friendly request will allow you to pass a "no trespassing" sign.
- Don't remove anything. *Anything.* How would you feel if that rusted gate hinge had been taken by the person visiting the site just before you? (*Exception:* Why not remove a film wrapper or an aluminum can, even if it's not yours? I was once allowed into a site closed to the public because the owner had observed me picking up other people's trash.)
- Take a camera you're familiar with and plenty of film.
- Don't take a metal detector. Although many people use them for harmless recreation, others carry them to look for items that can only be found by digging up a townsite, a foundation, a floor. Residents of ghost towns have had bad experiences with visitors using metal detectors and dislike the device as a consequence.
- Collect ghost town books. One book's weakness is another's strength. Naturally, I believe this book has several strengths; however, it does not include historical photographs. Comparing what a site looked like at the turn of the century with what you see now can make the visit more enjoyable, and some other books supply such photographs.

What to Look for at Ghost Town Sites

Ghost towns in California range from the dramatic and nearly intact to the devastated and virtually vanished. That certainly does not mean, however, that only the major sites are worth visiting; often the remote and deteriorated foundations at the end of a dirt trail offer a fulfillment and solitude that well-known (and perhaps more commercial) towns lack. And, after some practice, you will see more than a person who doesn't know what to look for at a sparse site.

As you might imagine, most California ghost towns are mining related. But not all—in this book you'll find railroad towns, a supply camp for nearby mines, a World War II relocation center, a site that was little more than a promoter's swindle, an aqueduct construction workers' town, and even a socialist colony. At nonmining sites, the remnants will be as varied as the cause of the town's existence: at a railroad town like Keeler, depots and railroad beds; at Berdoo Camp, solid foundations of a company town that housed workers on the aqueduct; and at Llano, the walls of dairy barns and remnants of irrigation ditches at a socialist workers' dream gone sour.

Mining towns are different. The least permanent are those, like the site of Potholes, at which only placer deposits were worked (for a definition of "placer" and other terms used in mining, see Appendix B). At such locales you will find little more than evidence of stream disturbance. More promising for ghost town enthusiasts are communities that formed around primary mineral deposits and had mills or smelters. There you should look for adits with waste dumps on hillsides and shafts with headframes on more level ground. The Randsburg area, for example, features some picturesque headframes.

Mills usually stand longer than residential or commercial buildings, because they were of heavier construction and more difficult to move or dismantle. Even if the mills themselves are gone, the sites they once occupied are often prominent since the mills were generally built into the sides of hills to minimize the amount of foundation work and take advantage of gravity in the milling process. One of the best mills in the West is at Skidoo; another outstanding mill can be found at the Lost Horse Mine; good examples of mill foundations are at Picacho.

Another photogenic structure is the occasional tramway, which transported ore from the mine or mill to a distant location, such as a point of debarkation. The best tramway remnants I have seen in the West stand at the Keane Wonder Mine. Two other fine tramways are at Cerro Gordo.

Heavy-duty buildings like smelters, ovens, and chimneys can stand for generations. Smelter foundations remain at Cerro Gordo and Swansea. You can see ovens at the Wildrose and the Cottonwood charcoal kilns. A dramatic chimney rises above the site of the mill at Panamint.

Residential, commercial, and municipal buildings—schools, churches, and the like—tend to survive longer if they are rock or stone. The remarkable American Hotel in Cerro Gordo is made of wood, and its existence is tenuous indeed. Fire, wind, a collapsing roof, or a bulldozer could level it in a moment. But the walls of the assay office at Providence, for example, should stand for dozens of decades if left alone. An adobe structure can endure for centuries *if* it has a roof. When the roof collapses, the building will deteriorate rapidly as rain washes down. As a result, the walls at such sites as Silver Lake, Ballarat, and the Araz Stage Station will not stand for long without protection.

Many of my favorite excursions have been highlighted by visits to cemeteries. Several things make cemeteries memorable: the varied sizes, materials, and designs of grave markers; the verses on the markers, mostly doggerel but occasionally eloquent—and certainly heartfelt; and, perhaps most importantly, the speculations on the lives of the people buried there—the unanswered puzzles that tombstones often pose. The cemetery at Calico, overlooked in the rush for the gift shops and amusement rides, has a desolate charm. The graveyard at Manzanar reminds us of a tragedy that must never be repeated. The graves of Jimmy Dayton and Shorty Harris are simple monuments to men who braved the toughest conditions that the United States has to offer. The Potholes cemetery has proved far more permanent than the town itself.

A ghost town, to me, is any site that has had a markedly decreased population from its peak, a town whose initial reason for settlement (such as a mine or a railroad) no longer keeps people in the community. A ghost town, then, can be completely deserted, like Hedges and Berdoo Camp; it can have a resident or two, like Keyesville and Ryan; or it can be a town with genuine signs of vitality, like Julian and Calico.

People in ghost towns are occasionally defensive, sometimes downright hostile. They may resent being considered a curiosity, and they have watched with fury as visitors have pillaged their hometowns. Can we blame them? On the other hand, some of the warmest, most generous people I have ever met live in these towns. It is your responsibility to assuage the doubters with polite assurances and to convince the friendly that you won't betray their affability by disturbing the remnants of the town in which they live. But don't ignore the residents, for if you go to an inhabited ghost town and meet only ghosts, you will have neglected the town's greatest treasure.

A WORD OF CAUTION ABOUT DIRECTIONS AND MAPS

Each of the following entries begins with directions that were accurate when the site was visited in the 1980s. Of course, changes can occur over the years; a new road could bypass the site, a locked gate could bar access, or, tragically, an entire site could be burned or razed.

The maps accompanying this book are not intended to replace topographic maps when sites are far from main roads. Their purpose is to give a clear picture of the towns' positions relative to main roads, larger towns, and other ghost town sites. The reader will need to use these maps in conjunction with the written directions for each entry and occasionally with a highway map or one or more topographic maps. A section at the end of each chapter tells the reader which topographic maps are the most helpful.

Southern California's Best
Ghost Towns

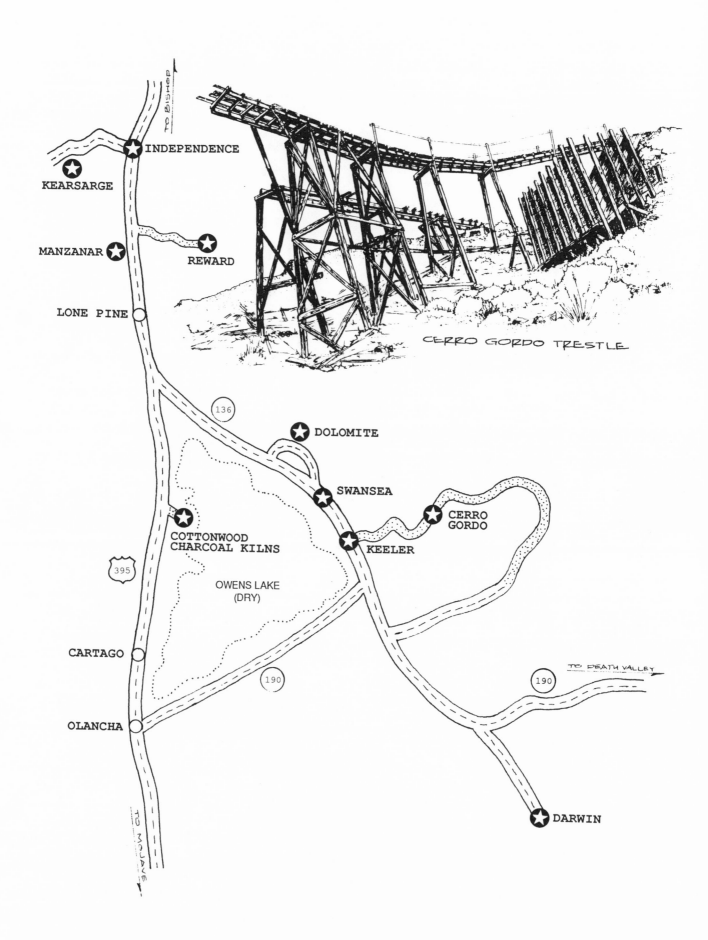

TO BISHOP

INDEPENDENCE

KEARSARGE

MANZANAR

REWARD

LONE PINE

CERRO GORDO TRESTLE

136

DOLOMITE

SWANSEA

COTTONWOOD
CHARCOAL KILNS

CERRO
GORDO

KEELER

395

OWENS LAKE
(DRY)

CARTAGO

TO DEATH VALLEY

190

190

OLANCHA

TO MOJAVE

DARWIN

1. Inyo Ghosts

Inyo County is an area of marked contrasts, from its fourteen-thousand-foot peaks to its wind-blown dry lakes. *Inyo* is an Indian word meaning "dwelling place of a great spirit," and that great spirit was once surrounded by natural beauty, abundant water and mineral wealth. But mining interests have removed most of the minerals, with several ghost towns standing as reminders of their efforts. The water was channeled—some would say "pirated"—for a thirsty Los Angeles. As Will Rogers put it, ". . . this was a wonderful valley with a quarter million acres of fruit and alfalfa. But Los Angeles had to have more water for its chamber of commerce to drink more toasts to its growth, more water to dilute its orange juice. . . . So, now this is the valley of desolation."

If it is a valley of desolation, it is at least a desolation of great beauty. And the contrasts continue in more than scenery. What was once a fruit- and nut-growing region is now arid. Where there once existed a frantic search for precious metals, a determined few still doggedly pursue the leftovers. For the ghost town hunter, there are contrasts as well: melancholy Manzanar, dusty Darwin, and spectacular Cerro Gordo.

Independence, a town you might use as a base (along with Lone Pine) as you visit the sites in this chapter, features important spots of historical interest, so spend a little time exploring it for its own sake. In 1861 Charles Putnam constructed a stone house 130 feet west of the historical landmark on the main street through town. Called, appropriately, Putnam's (and later Little Pine), Putnam's cabin served as a home, a trading post, a fort, and even a hospital in the early days of settlement of Owens Valley. In 1862 Lt. Col. George S. Evans established a fort about 2 miles north of Putnam's; he named it Camp Independence because it was commemorated on the Fourth of July. Built to provide military protection for the settlers to the area, the fort was occupied until 1877. You can still see some evidence of Camp Independence by driving north of town and turning right at the intersection where the road to the fish hatchery is on the left.

In 1866 Thomas Edwards laid out the present townsite and took the name of the nearby fort for the name of the town. In Independence today, in addition to the Putnam's cabin landmark, there are two places the visitor should be certain to see. One is the home of Mary Austin, whose 1903 book *Land of Little Rain* is a Western classic. The other is the Eastern California Museum, which features displays of settlers, Indians, and soldiers; excellent historical photographs of the area; and an outdoor display including buildings, wagons, and implements that were brought to the museum to give a representation of life in the early days of Owens Valley. There is no charge to visit the museum, but donations are accepted—and certainly deserved.

KEARSARGE

The only site of Kearsarge worth visiting (see text for explanation) is 9.5 miles west of Independence on the road to Onion Valley.

Actually, there were three places named Kearsarge, but the topographic map and most ghost town books show only the third, a train stop along the abandoned Carson and Colorado Railroad bed east of Independence. Nothing remains at the site (which at one point was renamed Citrus to avoid its being confused with the mine) except a fence and evidence of the abandoned McIver Canal. If you want to look anyway, drive east 4.3 miles on Mazourka Canyon Road (formerly Citrus Road) until the pavement ends.

A more rewarding visit is to an earlier Kearsarge. But first some background. Just west of Lone Pine are the Alabama Hills, named in 1863 by Confederate sympathizers who were crowing about the sinking of the Union warship *Hatteras* by the raider *Alabama.* Then Thomas Hill found gold in some quartz veins in a range north of the Alabama Hills in 1864, and Union sympathizers gained some topographic revenge on September 19 of that year when a new mining district was formed and was given the name Kearsarge, after the ship that recently had sunk the *Alabama* off the coast of France. The town that grew around the gold and silver deposits took the name of the mining district, and so did the mountain. The warship *Kearsarge,* incidentally, was named for a mountain in New Hampshire. The top producer in the Kearsarge District was the Rex Montis (Latin—"King of the Mountain") mine, which was in operation from 1875 to 1883, again in 1935, and once more in 1966. A forty-stamp mill was erected at the site of Kearsarge, but the gradual growth of the camp was ended in one night; on March 1, 1867, an avalanche smothered the town that at one time had been the largest settlement in the Owens Valley. It was never rebuilt.

Stone walls and foundations of Kearsarge blend with the rugged Sierras.

A second Kearsarge was, however, and its remains are 9.5 miles west of Independence and 3.5 miles beyond Grays Meadow Campground. There you can see, among the brush, definite rock foundations and faint outlines of walls as the scenic road to Onion Valley makes a switchback.

On your return trip to Independence, you should also examine the Inyo Mill, visible from the road 1.8 miles from the rock ruins of the second Kearsarge (and 7.7 miles west of Independence). Inside the mill is an arrastre, a very unusual sight inside a building of rather recent vintage.

MANZANAR

Manzanar is 5.8 miles south of Independence and 8.8 miles north of Lone Pine on U.S. 395.

Manzanar, "apple orchard" in Spanish, was originally the center in the Owens Valley for the fruit-growing industry. A post office was established in 1911, but the town began to dry up a year later when the Owens Valley Water Project took water from the area and diverted it to Los Angeles. This may seem an established fact now to Californians, but many people in Owens Valley still speak with great bitterness about the "theft" of their water. As W. A. Chalfant, respected Inyo County writer-historian, once put it, "The government held Owens Valley while Los Angeles skinned it."

So Manzanar's promising future was cut short. But that is only the beginning of the story—Manzanar became a place of genuine tragedy. After almost thirty years of neglect, the desolate place once again came to life in one of this country's sorriest episodes. On February 19, 1942, Executive Order 9066 commanded all persons of Japanese ancestry who lived on the West Coast to report, beginning on March 30 of that year, for transportation to "relocation centers" in areas that the government deemed

The Inyo Mill—with arrastre inside—near the road to Onion Valley

Pagoda-style guard houses at the entrance to Manzanar

to be nonstrategic during wartime. Ten such camps were placed in remote areas of California, Arizona, Idaho, Wyoming, Colorado. Utah, and Arkansas. In all, 120,313 people, most of them American citizens, lived for two and a half years in the internment camps; they were even kept there eighteen months longer than Secretary of War Henry. L. Stimson recommended. The apparent reason for this, according to the Commission on Wartime Relocation and Internment of Civilians in a report released in 1983, was purely political: President Roosevelt was concerned about the implications of releasing the internees before a national election. It was not until 1988 that the United States accepted any culpability in the matter. In that year, Congress passed legislation, signed by President Ronald Reagan, granting a monetary reparation to survivors of the internment camps.

The first of the camps to be completed was Manzanar, where eventually 10,000 people of Japanese descent came to live. Very little remains to indicate the size of Manzanar unless you look around. At first glance, all that seems to be there are gates and two guard houses (ironically, of oriental architecture), along with a California Historical Landmark plaque. The guard houses' interiors are filled with graffiti, many of them signatures of Japanese Americans who have visited the site, several identifying themselves as former Manzanar residents. And there is much more to see: just north of the site is an Inyo County maintenance yard, whose large shed is actually the most solid evidence of the internment camp, for the building was originally Manzanar's gymnasium and auditorium, complete with stage and projection booth. Beyond the gates and guard houses you can drive on several good dirt roads back into the actual dwelling area. There you will find, in this square-mile facility, evidence of streets, clearings for the tar-papered barracks that housed the families, and one touching attempt to make this bleak place a home. Among trees on the western end of the camp are the remnants of a small rock garden and pond that probably constituted the most beautiful spot in Manzanar. Just beyond is a small cemetery with a memorial tower. Its inscription translates as "the monument of comforting the soul," or "the monument for the consolation of the spirits."

On the south end of the facility, across a wash, are more permanent foundations, concrete walks, and a barbecue pit. I wondered why this area would be obviously so much better constructed than the

Memorial at the Manzanar cemetery

rest of the camp. Then I surmised the sad truth, which was later substantiated by a worker at the Inyo maintenance yard: that relatively luxurious section of camp wasn't for internees at all. Their guards lived there.

Two more areas remain to be explored at Manzanar, and not too many people know about them. Drive north from the guard houses to the Manzanar-Reward Road. Turn east, and shortly you will come to a flat, obviously cleared space. This was the Manzanar Airport. Once when I was there the Inyo County Sheriff's Department was using the old runways to practice chase techniques. Continue on the main dirt road, cross a canal, and go beyond the power line .2 miles, where there is a turnoff at a fence. South of that fence .9 miles are the considerable remains of the Manzanar sewage treatment plant, including foundations of buildings, a large water tank, and an assortment of concrete treatment tanks. This plant was one of the most modern sewage plants in the country when it was built for the internment camp, according to a lifelong resident of the valley. At least it's nice to know that the United States was going to considerable expense for treatment of the sewage of the American citizens who were living in the tar-paper shacks. The California Landmark plaque reads: "May the injustices and

The Inyo Mountains dwarf the large hopper and tramway terminals at Reward.

humiliation suffered here as a result of hysteria, racism, and economic exploitation never emerge again."

REWARD

Reward is 5.3 miles east of U.S. 395 on the Manzanar-Reward Road, which is just north of the site of Manzanar.

The Eclipse Mine, discovered in 1860, was very likely the first location of a mine in Owens Valley. Later called the Brown Monster, it and its companion mine, the Reward, provided the largest source of gold—along with modest amounts of silver, lead, and copper—in Owens Valley. The mines were active until 1936. The International Recovery Company was doing some work in the early 1980s, but the site was deserted when I visited it again in 1988. The town of Reward was a trading center for the mines in the valley and had a post office from 1900 to 1906.

From the entrance to the property you can get a good view, especially with binoculars or a telescope, of about five structures up in the canyon of the Inyo Mountains, including a water tank, a tram terminus, and a long wooden hopper near the Reward and Brown Monster mines.

DOLOMITE

Drive south 2.4 miles from Lone Pine. There at the intersection is a visitors' center well worth a stop. The turnoff to Dolomite is 3.2 miles east of that intersection on state route 136. The town is 3.7 miles on up the road.

The chalkish, dusty-looking foothills of the Inyo Mountains mark the location of the mineral dolomite, a carbonate of lime and magnesia. In 1888 the Inyo Marble Company opened a quarry at this site northwest of Keeler to extract dolomite marble, some of which adorns buildings in San Francisco. More recently used in decorative roofing, dolomite from this quarry was also utilized in the terrazzo flooring of the Los Angeles International Airport. A

Dolomite—the "adobe" building to the left is actually wood frame, part of a movie set. The general store was at least partly enhanced by Hollywood.

Vacant residences at Dolomite

map showing the stops of the Carson and Colorado Railroad identifies this location as "Inyo," no doubt for the name of the parent marble company; most current maps do not denote the site at all, and I was unable to ascertain when the site became known as Dolomite.

Currently four good ghost town buildings and a couple of newer structures comprise the site. All the old structures are weathered wood, and their shingled roofs lose something to each strong wind. At least part of the site was "improved" by a movie company, and the best building, with a faded sign that once said "General Store," is a false front whose authenticity is definitely questionable. It has a strange roof line, with a series of boards jutting straight up; it is distinctly out of sync, almost as if Federico Fellini had made a Western there. Next door to the store is a building more discernible as part of a movie set: it's supposed to be adobe, but its framework is wood.

SWANSEA

Swansea is 12.6 miles (including the side trip to Dolomite) southeast of Lone Pine along state route 136.

The town of Swansea was built in 1870 under the direction of James Brady, who had assumed operation of the Owens Lake Silver-Lead Furnace that had been constructed the previous year. Named for the famous smelting site of Swansea, Wales, the town offered the support facilities for the smelting and shipping operations that had become necessary because of the size of ore discoveries in the Cerro Gordo area. Swansea was also headquarters of the Owens Lake Silver-Lead Company, the rival to Mortimer Belshaw's operation in Cerro Gordo (see Cerro Gordo entry).

The owner of the site at this writing is Jody Stewart, who is planning to restore and revive Swansea. That may be down the line a bit, since currently her primary efforts are at Cerro Gordo. At the Swansea townsite are the Wells Fargo stage station, with walls of dolomite from the nearby hills; James Brady's adobe house, which has several later addi-

Wells Fargo stage station at Swansea

All that remains of the Owens Lake Silver-Lead Furnace at Swansea

tions to it; a wooden shed that was perhaps Brady's carriage house; an adobe and stone building that might have been for storage of food and wine; and a wooden bunkhouse, almost certainly from a later era. Also on the property is a cistern, which pumps water from a depth of only ten feet and is the source of the water at Cerro Gordo, hauled by truck the 12 miles up to the townsite.

Across the road on the south side of the highway is a small building and a California Historical Landmark for the 1869 Owens Lake Silver-Lead Furnace. The rock remnants of the furnace, charred black on the inside, are a short distance away.

The white, parched flat that is now Owens Dry Lake was in 1869 a lake of one hundred square miles with a maximum depth of thirty feet. Bullion from the Cerro Gordo strike was shipped across Owens Lake on the steamer *Bessie Brady,* launched in June 1872, to Cartago and then on to Los Angeles by fourteen-mule teams. On the return trip from Cartago to Swansea, the steamer would be laden with lumber, machinery, food, liquor, and grain. The *Bessie Brady,* which was named for co-owner James Brady's daughter, measured eighty-five feet long with a sixteen-foot beam, was propelled by a twenty-horsepower engine, and could haul seventy tons of freight.

The smelter shut down in 1874 after a cloudburst buried much of Swansea and filled the smelter with mud. The Owens Lake Silver-Lead Company was at that time embroiled in an expensive legal dispute with Mortimer Belshaw and could not afford to rebuild.

Northwest of the townsite along the highway is sparse evidence of the salt tramway that once climbed across the mountains, passed near the small community of Daisy, and dropped down into the Saline Valley.

KEELER

Keeler is 3 miles southeast of Swansea and 15.6 miles from Lone Pine on state route 136.

"Keeler—End of the Line," states the E Clampus Vitus plaque across the street from the old two-story railroad station. I'll bet that some adolescents growing up in Keeler would agree. Although the town has some spectacular but stark views of Owens Lake, Cerro Gordo Peak, and Mount Whitney, Keeler is a rather dusty, forlorn-looking place itself. The Sierra Talc Company building is the largest structure in town and has been a favorite subject of artists. Nearby, obscured by foliage, is the former schoolhouse. Near Owens Dry Lake is the Keeler dry swimming pool, closed and locked up when I was there on a scorching summer day. Across the street from the train station are two frame buildings that I could only call "Siamese twin" architecture (see photo, page 11). Adjoining the stores is a concrete wall with a fading sign touting "Famous A.B.C. Beer." I guess fame is relative. Heading northeast from Keeler is the road to Cerro Gordo (see following entry), and east along the highway is the Keeler cemetery, which features some old markers in a rather barren setting.

The "End of the Line" plaque refers to the Carson and Colorado Railroad, begun on May 1, 1880, which extended from Mound House, Nevada (on the Carson River), to Keeler. Planners intended to send the line to Fort Mohave on the Colorado River (hence the railroad's name). The completion of the 293-mile route to Keeler in 1883 meant that commerce in the Owens Valley would primarily travel north toward San Francisco rather than south to Los Angeles, but by the time the line reached Keeler, the principal reason for commerce—Cerro Gordo—had shut down. When financier Darius O. Mills traveled his Carson and Colorado Railroad on July 12, 1883, for the end-of-track inspection, he surveyed the scene with a sombre silence and intoned, "Gentlemen, we either built it three hundred miles too long or three hundred years too soon." He sold it in 1900, at a great loss, to Southern Pacific. The last train operated on the line on April 29, 1960.

Before the arrival of the railroad, Keeler had been known since the 1870s as Cerro Gordo Landing, a shipping point for the prosperous mines in the

Sierra Talc Company plant at Keeler

mountains above. Forty years later, an aerial tramway was constructed from the Union Shaft at Cerro Gordo all the way to Keeler.

According to author and railroad historian David F. Myrick, the original rail stop was called Hawley, because the C & C ended at Hawley's Mill, which

Keeler—identical commercial buildings

later closed. The town was renamed Keeler in 1882 for Julius M. Keeler, who reopened the mill. Keeler was a '49er who also fought in the Civil War, where he earned the rank of captain. According to Erwin Gudde's *California Place Names,* he was later the manager of the Inyo Marble Company quarry (see Dolomite entry). Keeler's mill was fueled with wood sent by barge across Owens Lake from Cottonwood Canyon after Keeler had repaired the canyon's old flume (see Cottonwood entry).

Now the mill is gone, the tramway is gone, and the railroad is gone. For some, surely, it is "Keeler— End of the Line."

CERRO GORDO

Two routes take you to Cerro Gordo. The first, shorter but quite steep and mountainous, is to drive 7.7 miles up the old Yellow Grade Road (so named for the area's yellow shale) that begins at the historical landmark sign along state route 136 in Keeler. The second route comes up the back from the Saline Valley. If you have a car with usual clearance and sufficient power, the first, more direct route is much better under normal road conditions.

No other ghost town within 150 miles even comes close. Bodie has more buildings, but it has some-

Cerro Gordo townsite—Union Mine hoist house and dumps above; Louis Gordon house (with dormer window) at right center; Beaudry store at center of photo, with Belshaw house facing it

thing else Cerro Gordo does not—too many people. Once home to some 4,700 people, Cerro Gordo is California's best true ghost town.

The silver-lead bonanza in the mountains near Owens Lake made Los Angeles a city. If that seems like an impossible exaggeration, consider the Los Angeles *News* in 1870: "To this city, the Owens River trade is invaluable. What Los Angeles is, is mainly due to it." Here was a classic cause-and-effect relationship. In 1865, Pablo Flores and two other Mexicans found rich silver ore deposits near Cerro Gordo Peak (*cerro gordo* means "big" or "fat hill" in Spanish, which refers either to the rounded shapes of the mountains or the fact that they were "fat"—meaning "rich"—in ore). Because of the remarkable extent of the vein, a shipping route was established through the Owens Val-

ley that gave the sleepy pueblo of Los Angeles the bulk of the transportation and supply business; hence the remark in the Los Angeles *News*.

A year after the discovery of the silver-lead deposits, the Lone Pine Mining District was formed. Two years later, San Francisco mining engineer Mortimer W. Belshaw arrived at Cerro Gordo; he quickly recognized the potential of the operation and the way to get a lock on it. Belshaw understood a chain of events that, once controlled, could result in a possible monopoly and enormous profits. The shipping of silver ore would be most efficient if smelted at the site; smelting of silver requires lead; lead is in galena; and galena deposits were abundant in Cerro Gordo. So Belshaw bought into the Union Mine (for silver and lead), eventually owned two of the three smelters at the site, constructed a toll road using the only reasonable access route from Owens Lake, and controlled the water supply. He and Victor Beaudry, who had arrived even earlier than Belshaw and who owned the Cerro Gordo store, became partners; the two of them dominated Cerro Gordo through its short but very prosperous life. How prosperous? Between 1868 and 1875 approximately $13,000,000 in silver-lead bullion was shipped from the Cerro Gordo smelters, making the mines the greatest producers of those metals in California's history.

The person responsible for transporting the huge quantities of bullion was Remi Nadeau, whose mule-team freight wagons traveled down the treacherous Yellow Grade Road—Belshaw's toll road—and skirted the north shore of Owens Lake. They then headed across the Mojave Desert, into Los Angeles, and finally to the port of San Pedro. From there the silver and lead shipment was taken by paddle-wheel steamboats to San Francisco. By 1870 Nadeau's freight teams were consuming the surplus barley grown in Los Angeles County, and his return trips included practically all the foodstuffs that the farmers of the San Fernando Valley could produce. Cerro Gordo, with an 1870 population of 2,000, was making Southern California come alive.

Production became so overwhelming—as many as 400 bars weighing about eighty-five pounds each in a twenty-four-hour period—that the freight teams could not keep up. Nadeau's great-great-grandson, author Remi Nadeau, says that at one point 30,000 ingots had accumulated for shipment. Miners, an imaginative lot who always seem to find a use for just about everything, stacked the ingots to make cabins.

In 1872 the shipping route was shortened considerably by initiating steamboat runs across Owens Lake to Cartago, on the western shore. In the following year a route to Stevens Wharf was added to pick up the lumber and charcoal from Cottonwood Creek (see Cottonwood Charcoal Kilns entry). The first steamer, the *Bessie Brady,* helped the logistics of the shipping problems considerably, and in 1874 Remi Nadeau's teams delivered more than $4,000,000 worth of silver to Los Angeles.

But by 1877 the mines began to play out. The Union Works burned and were abandoned in 1879. The last load of bullion was shipped the following year. In 1882, the *Bessie Brady* burned, and in 1883 the railroad reached Keeler (see preceding en-

try) only to have the days of prosperity over and the reason for the railroad past. Keeler became the end of the line. Cerro Gordo's post office somehow managed to stay open until 1895.

Cerro Gordo came back to life in 1911 when zinc was discovered by Louis Gordon and the mines became the principal source for high-quality zinc in the United States. Two aerial tramways were built in the next few years to transport the ore, one going directly from the Union Shaft all the way to Keeler and the other from the Morning Star Mine down to a terminus on the Yellow Grade Road. The tramways didn't require engines because the weight of the ore down the steep grade was powerful enough to carry supplies loaded in at Keeler back up to Cerro Gordo in the empty buckets. The biggest problem was braking the cable and buckets as they lurched down the hill. The zinc operations continued into the 1930s, when once again the town drifted into inactivity. The tram house and machinery were dismantled in 1959 and relocated at mines in Candelaria, Nevada.

Ghost town seekers have had varied success in getting into Cerro Gordo over the last couple of decades. Sometimes they have been greeted with friendliness and generosity, as I was in 1982 by then-caretakers Myles and Erna Veltman. At other times "no trespassing" signs were up at the base of the grade and the reception was less than friendly, depending upon who was the caretaker, who was doing work on the mine, what the current politics were between Cerro Gordo owners and Inyo County officials, and other such variables.

At this writing, the news is very good, because currently Cerro Gordo is in the dedicated and capable hands of Jody Stewart, who, along with general manager Mike Patterson, is working to preserve and restore the townsite. The two of them have made incredible progress since I first saw the site, especially when one considers that at 8,500 feet there is only so much work that can be done during the winter months. Their goal is to make Cerro Gordo interesting but not too touristy; so far, they are succeeding admirably. There is no specific admission charge, but I strongly recommend a contribution for their efforts, since without them the site would no doubt fall prey to vandals and the elements—perhaps the former more than the latter. I suggest the following etiquette. Phone or write to make arrangements for your visit (619-876-4154;

P.O. Box 221, Keeler CA 93530); respect the antiquity of the site by not removing anything at all; and bring your own water, as Jody and Mike have to haul theirs in from Swansea, down on the shore of Owens Lake.

The first evidence of Cerro Gordo will appear as you drive up the road from Keeler. There, near a switchback, is the terminus of the tramway from the Morning Star Mine; the mine itself is not visible from this point but can be viewed, perched high on the side of the mountain, from the Keeler cemetery along state route 136. Not far beyond this terminus the road really becomes steep, climbing from Keeler, at 3,609 feet, to over 8,500 feet in less than eight miles, and much of that altitude gain comes in the last three miles. The road is certainly negotiable, but not for the faint of heart.

The first structure as you enter Cerro Gordo will be on your left—the stone chimney of Victor Beaudry's smelter. Beyond it on the same side of the road stand a shop, a bunkhouse, and an assay office. To the right are four classic wooden buildings on a rise just above the road—an icehouse, a screened-in coolhouse (identified as a gazebo in most books) for vegetables and fruits, the magnificent two-story American Hotel (dating from 1871), and another structure, perhaps a residence or an office. The American Hotel is the best of the group—indeed, one of the better buildings of the Old West. Still inside are tables, curtains, a bunk or two, and a giant cookstove. On the hills behind the American Hotel stand several miners' shacks.

The road continues up the hill and then forks, the

Screened-in coolhouse for food storage stands to the left of the icehouse at Cerro Gordo.

right road separating three residences. The largest is the Gordon House, which dates from the early part of this century and is now the beautifully restored home of Jody Stewart. To the left of the Gordon House are two houses, the larger of which is the oldest standing building in Cerro Gordo, built in 1868. Now housing a photo studio complete with era costumes, it was originally the home of Mortimer Belshaw, the leading entrepreneur during Cerro Gordo's boom days. Directly across from Belshaw's is a tin false front that probably was the Beaudry store, which now features a collection of mining implements and various household items. Above Beaudry's store are the dilapidated cribs of an old brothel. Standing dramatically behind is a rickety trestle, all that remains of the tramway that took the zinc from the Union Mine and sent it to Keeler. If you stand near the top of the trestle and look towards Keeler, you can get a feeling of the enormity of that enterprise.

The Union hoist house, with its dumps looming over Cerro Gordo, still has all sorts of old machinery in it, including a giant winch, furnaces, and headframe (but be careful around its 900-foot main shaft). The Morning Star Mine, which is 1.1 miles southeast of town on a jeep road that will likely be off limits to you, features a couple of buildings and remnants of its old tramway whose terminus you passed on the Yellow Grade Road on the way up. And over the hill from Cerro Gordo, on the road to the Saline Valley, are the ruins of the Owens Lake smelter, a competitor that Belshaw tried to put out of business more than once.

On my first visit to Cerro Gordo, while I was

American Hotel at Cerro Gordo

Victor Beaudry's company store at Cerro Gordo, with tram trestle in the background

Tram trestle from the Union Shaft at Cerro Gordo

View from the trestle past Beaudry's store and the American Hotel in Cerro Gordo. The road is the old Yellow Grade that comes up from Keeler.

The Morning Star Mine, south of Cerro Gordo townsite

standing on the trestle of the tramway from the Union Mine, I had the most momentarily terrifying experience in all my years of exploring ghost towns. I was peering through my telephoto lens down to the Owens Valley, when suddenly into focus came the nose of a jet fighter heading straight at me as it careened up the canyon. It screeched over the townsite and left me gasping and holding on to the shaking trestle. The caretaker at the time, Myles Veltman, told me that the jets come through frequently, shaking the whole town. This might be the only site in the country at which a major threat to its preservation is jet fighters. They should be prohibited from coming near such a national treasure.

Cerro Gordo significantly affected California's history. It stands as one of the very best ghost towns in the West, a clear reminder of our past. Jody Stewart and Mike Patterson deserve our admiration and support.

DARWIN

Darwin is 23 miles southeast of Keeler.

A dusty, sleeping town now, Darwin was once the trading center for the mining activity that began in earnest in the early 1870s in the nearby Argus and Coso ranges. The town was named for Fort Tejon rancher Dr. Darwin French, who named a wash after himself when he was in the area in about 1860. Eventually his name was also attached to a canyon, a falls, and the town. Dr. French found several silver ledges in the Cosos (*coso* means "fire" in Paiute), but what he was really looking for was the famous "lost" Gunsight Lode.

The Gunsight went back to 1850, when Jim Martin of the Georgian "Bugsmashers" party that was heading for the California goldfields hiked into a canyon seeking water and found not water, but abundant silver. He carried out of Death Valley some of the silver-lead ore and had it made into a gunsight. The source of that silver was never again found, although it is safe to say that someone is out searching for the Gunsight Lode at this moment. According to author Richard Lingenfelter, however, if they're looking for the Lost Gunsight in the Argus or Coso ranges, they aren't even close, since, if it exists at all, it's likely to be found in the Panamint Mountains.

Real riches were found in the area of Darwin beginning in late 1874. The new boomtown of Darwin almost immediately gained a reputation for violence: the sheriff pointed out once that of the 124 graves in the local cemetery, 122 were the result of the use of a gun or knife. By 1875, the town had two smelters, 200 frame houses, and a population

Looking from the Morning Star Mine down to Owens Dry Lake and the Sierra Nevada Range. Four tram supports are visible heading down the mountain. Parts of the Yellow Grade Road can also be seen. The small settlement at left center of the photograph is Keeler.

of 700 (some estimates have put the figure twice as high). The best saloon, the Centennial, featured cut-glass chandeliers and a billiard table of the same pattern found in San Francisco's Palace Hotel. One of the smartest people in Darwin was Victor Beaudry, who earlier had been one of the two prime movers of Cerro Gordo. Beaudry had learned his lesson well from his former Cerro Gordo partner, Mortimer Belshaw—get control of a commodity that is essential to the survival of the camp. He purchased the only large spring and became known as the Water King.

In the best times, the mines in the area kept three smelters busy, but by 1913 only one smelter was operating. Actually, the town had been moribund for decades before that; Darwin had begun to empty

with the rise of the towns of Bodie and Mammoth in 1878. Between 1874 and 1951, however, Darwin accumulated some impressive statistics: 5,914 ounces of gold; 7,630,492 ounces of silver; 117,566,900 pounds of lead; 52,124,947 pounds of zinc; and 1,489,396 pounds of copper.

Two attractions bring visitors to Darwin today. Rock hounds are interested in the crystallized mineral specimens to be found in mine dumps (*Desert Magazine,* February 1963, has a detailed description of favorite sites), and ghost town enthusiasts like the buildings. At the foot of Mount Ophir are the considerable remains, marked by "no trespassing" signs, of the Anaconda company town. Built in the mid-1940s, it is considerably larger than the rest of Darwin. From the road into town you can

The Outpost at Darwin

clearly see the boxlike bachelor quarters in the company town. Two larger buildings at the mine site were a school and a hospital.

Several buildings in Darwin itself are worth photographing. At the main crossroads in town are the Outpost Shell—complete with gravity-feed pumps—and several wooden false fronts. One, built in 1876, has a sign saying that it was used as the schoolhouse from 1900 to 1917. On Market Street stands a museum containing mining relics, photographs, historic documents, local periodicals, and even Dr. Darwin French's medical kit. Museum

Darwin false front that once served as a schoolhouse

hours are irregular; you might phone ahead (619-876-5469) to arrange a visit.

COTTONWOOD CHARCOAL KILNS

The Cottonwood charcoal kilns stand 14.4 miles south of Lone Pine on U.S. 395. A California Historical Landmark sign directs you to the site, which is 1 mile east of the highway.

The incredibly rich silver-lead deposits at Cerro Gordo affected the history of the entire Owens Lake area. Swansea, Keeler, and Cartago, for example, all owe their existence either directly or indirectly to the smelting or transporting of the bullion from Cerro Gordo. And the two remarkable kilns standing near the west shore of Owens Lake attest to another necessity associated with the mines—the operation's insatiable need for lumber and fuel wood.

The Wildrose charcoal kilns (see entry, Chapter 2) are more spectacular than these kilns on the edge

Cottonwood charcoal kilns near Owens Dry Lake

of Owens Lake, but they are so different from each other that I would certainly recommend a visit here as well. The Wildrose kilns owe their well-preserved state largely to the fact that they were constructed of stone, while the more delicate Cottonwood kilns have been scorched, sand-blown, and melted because they are made of fragile clay bricks covered by a clay mud plaster. They now look more like something that a child might construct on a busy day at a Pacific beach—only on a much larger scale—than like the utilitarian tool of a businessman in the last century.

In 1873 Colonel Sherman Stevens constructed a sawmill on Cottonwood Creek, near the abundant supply of wood in Cottonwood Canyon, and built a flume to carry both uncut wood and lumber to connect with the supply route to the silver-lead mines in Cerro Gordo. The wood was put into the kilns and made into charcoal, and the charcoal and lumber were then hauled to Stevens Wharf, where they were put aboard the steamer *Bessie Brady* (and, for a short time beginning in 1877, the *Mollie Stevens*). The steamer took the cargo across Owens Lake, and from there mule teams hauled it up to the mines at Cerro Gordo. The lumber was used for buildings and for timbering the mine, and the charcoal fueled the smelters.

Capsule Summary

MAJOR SITES

Cerro Gordo—rich in remains and scenery, one of the best sites in the West

Manzanar—fascinating site if you take the time to explore

SECONDARY SITES

Dolomite—photogenic buildings amid desolate beauty

Keeler—several interesting structures in a living town

Darwin—many weathered buildings, most occupied

MINOR SITES

Swansea—several historic buildings

Reward—mine buildings up the canyon and evidence of recent habitation

Cottonwood Charcoal Kilns—deteriorating historic landmark

Kearsarge—foundations and a mill

ROAD CONDITIONS

Cerro Gordo—steep unpaved road that could be treacherous in bad weather

Manzanar, Reward, Dolomite, Cottonwood Charcoal Kilns—dirt roads for passenger cars

All other sites—paved roads

TRIP SUGGESTIONS

TRIP 1: Using Independence or Lone Pine (approximately 225 miles from Los Angeles and 375 from San Francisco) as your base, you can visit all the sites in this chapter in two leisurely paced

TOPOGRAPHIC MAP INFORMATION FOR CHAPTER ONE: INYO GHOSTS
(For map-reading assistance, consult Appendix A.)

Town	Topo Map Name	Size	Year	Importance*
Kearsarge 1, 2	Kearsarge Peak	7½'	1985	2
Kearsarge 3	Bee Springs Canyon	7½'	1982	3
Manzanar	Manzanar	7½'	1982	2
Reward	Union Wash	7½'	1982	2
Dolomite	Dolomite	7½'	1987 prv[a]	3
Swansea	Dolomite	7½'	1987 prv[a]	3
Keeler	Keeler	7½'	1987 prv[a]	3
Cerro Gordo	Cerro Gordo Peak	7½'	1987 prv[a]	2
Darwin	Darwin	7½'	1987 prv[a]	2
Cottonwood Charcoal Kilns	Bartlett	7½'	1987 prv[a]	3

[a]—provisional edition (see Appendix A, "Distinguishing Characteristics")

*1—essential to find and/or enjoy site to fullest
2—helpful but not essential
3—unnecessary to find and enjoy site

days. The total round-trip mileage from Independence to all sites is about 161 miles.

TRIP 2: Combine sites in this chapter with those in Chapter Two. Death Valley is 121 miles southeast of Independence.

TRIP 3: Combine sites in this chapter with those in Chapter Three. The Randsburg area is 108 miles south of Independence, and the Lake Isabella ghost towns are 129 miles to the southwest.

2. The Spirits of Death Valley

The ominous appellation "Death Valley" was probably bestowed by a member of the '49er Bennett-Arcan party as he remembered the death of companion Richard Culverwell, the first documented casualty of the valley. As they looked back on its perilous, parched expanse, the survivor is reported to have said, "Good-bye, Death Valley." Another assessment of the place came in 1861, when Death Valley was described as "a vast and deep pit of many gloomy wonders" by a member of the Boundary Commission. One who likely would have agreed is a miner named Coffin (!), who shared that morbid respect for the valley. In a probably apocryphal tale, he wrote home dolefully that he was employed on the graveyard shift at the Cemetery Mine, Skull Gulch, Funeral Range, overlooking Death Valley.

To be sure, Death Valley still can pose considerable dangers to unwary travelers; after all, it is the driest place in the United States and the hottest in the Western Hemisphere. Yet I find it to be a place not of "gloomy wonders" but of unspeakable beauty and astonishing variety. Its name may conjure up visions of barren flatlands, but in reality Death Valley offers much, much more. It deserves investigation on a number of fronts—geology, flora and fauna, and history, to name three. A good book for the ghost town explorer to have is Stanley W. Paher's *Death Valley Ghost Towns,* which includes historical photographs that make good comparisons to the sites today. The landmark book for the valley is Richard Lingenfelter's *Death Valley and the Amargosa: A Land of Illusion* (see Bibliography). A source cited frequently in this chapter, Lingenfelter's work is the first complete annotated telling of the Death Valley story, and it is excellent reading.

Along with ghost towns, this chapter will suggest some other spots of related interest, such as mines, landmarks, and other historic sites.

Area One: On the Valley Floor

DEATH VALLEY RANCH

Death Valley Ranch (Scotty's Castle) stands 45 miles north of Stovepipe Wells Village.

Scotty's Castle is, deservedly, one of the most frequently visited spots in Death Valley. You should not pass it up merely because everybody else is

Death Valley Ranch—"Scotty's Castle"

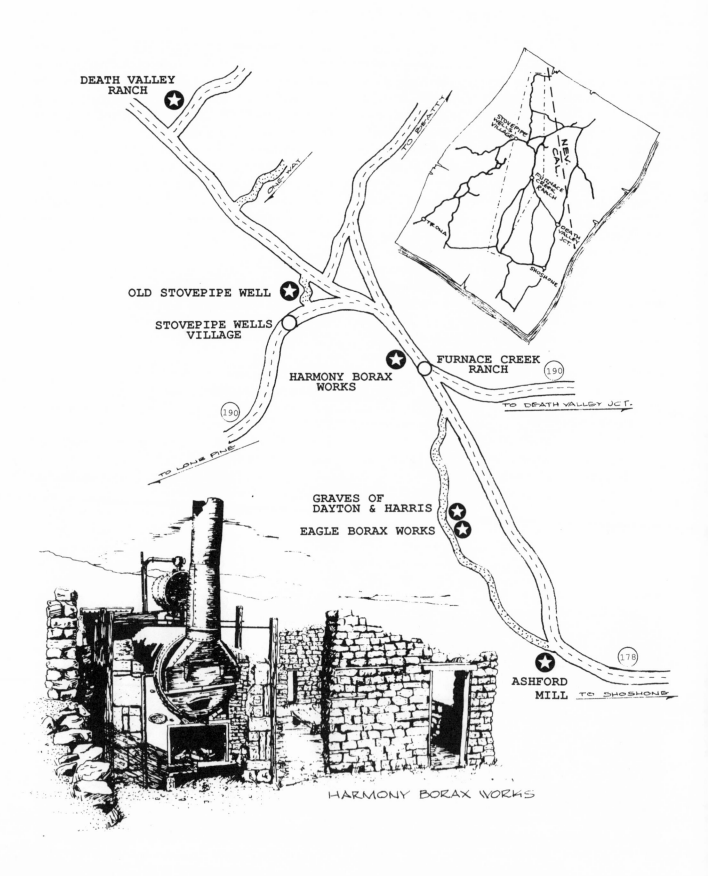

DEATH VALLEY
RANCH

TO BEATTY

ONE WAY

OLD STOVEPIPE WELL

STOVEPIPE WELLS
VILLAGE

HARMONY BORAX
WORKS

FURNACE CREEK
RANCH

(190)

(190)

TO DEATH VALLEY JCT.

TO LONE PINE

GRAVES OF
DAYTON & HARRIS

EAGLE BORAX WORKS

(178)

ASHFORD
MILL   TO SHOSHONE

HARMONY BORAX WORKS

going there, although I admit to having had that temptation. A fifty-minute tour takes you through the home that Walter E. Scott, "Death Valley Scotty," made famous, despite the fact that it wasn't his. If the tour leaves you desiring to know more about Scotty, the definitive—and fascinating—source to read is Hank Johnston's *Death Valley Scotty: The Fastest Con in the West* (see Bibliography). Johnston's book contains a thorough biography, rare photographs, maps, and reproductions of memorabilia from Scotty's life.

Although Death Valley Ranch isn't a ghost town, its most famous inhabitant is so much a part of the story, and his exploits so cover the terrain, that to omit Death Valley Scotty from this chapter would be to overlook a major part of the Valley's history, or at least of its hype. His original camp was in the southern section of the Valley, the Castle is in the northern, he held court to the east in Rhyolite, and he so captivated the press of Los Angeles that one would think L.A. was on the western fringe of Death Valley.

Walter Scott was born in Cynthiana, Kentucky, probably in 1872. As a young man he appeared in Buffalo Bill Cody's Wild West Show, but he left it in 1902 after a dispute with Cody, who saw him watching a parade in New York City in which Scotty should have been riding.

So Walter Scott headed West and settled in Death Valley, where he claimed he found a fabulous gold mine. But he needed capital to work it. Scotty's original backer was Julian M. Gerard, who had been conned into staking him when Scott had shown Gerard two specimens that Scott's wife, Ella Josephine McCarthy Milius Scott (nicknamed "Jack"), had been given in Cripple Creek, Colorado. Gerard received a number of letters from Scott reporting wild successes, nuggets, requests for money—but no return on his investment. One time Scotty headed East with "nuggets" to give Gerard, only to have them "stolen." But he kept insisting that his mine in Death Valley, supposedly located somewhere near Scott's Camp Holdout (not far from where the Ashford Mill ruins now stand), was loaded with paying ore. It is from accounts like the one above that we get a glimpse of Scotty as a "prospector." As Pete Aguereberry, longtime resident of Death Valley put it, all Walter Scott ever minded was other people's pockets.

And yet people continued to back him. In 1905, Los Angeles mining engineer E. Burdon Gaylord staked Scott to the cost of hiring the "Coyote Special," a chartered train that torpedoed across the country from Los Angeles to Chicago in the then-record time of forty-four hours and fifty-five minutes, breaking the previous record by almost eight hours and traveling as fast as 106 miles per hour at times. Scotty's train captivated the nation, and he became a national figure, although he was merely a passenger. Speculation is that Gaylord probably underwrote the trip because he was desperately looking for a buyer for his Big Bell Mine and wanted spectacular public attention for Death Valley. Actually, of course, the enterprise had nothing to do with mining gold, but rather with mining public opinion.

Up to this point Walter Scott seems to have been little more than a fellow with a definite flair for the dramatic and only a trace of larceny. That changed in February 1906 with the so-called "Battle of Wingate Pass." Albert M. Johnson, a Chicago financier, was interested in backing Walter Scott in his gold-mining venture, so he joined two other men who were to travel to Scott's famous, elusive mine in Death Valley to assess the value of the properties. Scotty, naturally, wanted the backing but was understandably hesitant to have his mine examined, since it didn't exist.

Five men of Scott's choosing came along on the expedition, ostensibly to assist in driving the animals and packing supplies. Two of his hirelings, Jack Brody and Bill Keys, were sent ahead to "scout for danger"; their real purpose was to set up a mock ambush to scuttle the tour. They opened fire on the party and accidentally hit Scotty's brother Warner. Scott rode out toward the direction of the gunfire shouting, "Stop the shooting! You've hit Warner!" Of course, that gave away the ruse. Nevertheless, despite arrests, lawsuits, and considerable scandal, all charges were dropped in the scheme, primarily for lack of evidence. Even as gossip about the incident played to great interest in the Los Angeles papers, Scotty himself played to full houses in a theatrical production about himself called *King of the Desert Mine,* starring Walter Scott, "Sphinx of the American Desert."

The surprising thing about the "Battle of Wingate Pass" (it wasn't, of course, a battle, and it wasn't in—only near—Wingate Pass) was that despite its exposure as a hoax (Bill Keys admitted as much), Albert Johnson still wanted in as a backer of Walter Scott. Gerard, who gave Scott his original stake and who had paid out thousands of dollars without seeing any return at all, was no doubt happy to have someone else come forward to take over the expense, while Gerard still was guaranteed a portion of any findings. The partnership with Albert Johnson was certainly the best thing that ever happened to Scotty—it set him up for life.

A couple of other incidents give an insight into the kind of man Walter Scott was, behind all the publicity and intrigue. Once during a visit to Rhyolite, Nevada, Scotty was punched in the eye by Alva D. Myers, the "Father of Goldfield." Scotty waited quite a while until Myers thought the incident had been forgotten and then invited the unsuspecting Myers to Death Valley to show him Scotty's mine. He took Myers to a spot near the old Eagle Borax Works (see entry, Chapter 2) and abandoned him for seven days in the desert heat while Scotty went up into the Panamint Mountains to cool comfort. If that sounds like an even payback, consider that Scotty left Myers, all right, but he left his own wife, Jack, down in the sweltering heat as well. Jack, incidentally, spent most of their married life in Los Angeles or Reno. Small wonder.

In 1908 Scott admitted to being part of an operation that high-graded gold ore in Goldfield, serving as a fence for the ore that had been stolen by miners working for large companies. He could, naturally, take ore in for assaying and then sell it by simply claiming it was from his famous, mysterious mine. Much of the myth and mystery of Walter "Death Valley Scotty" Scott evaporated when, in a court appearance in 1912 that stemmed from the Wingate Pass debacle, Scotty confessed that his mine in Death Valley was all a hoax and that he lived off the grubstakes from Johnson and Gerard.

So why did Albert Johnson continue to pour money into a nonexistent mine and, in such an unlikely place as Death Valley, eventually build one of America's most famous private residences? Johnson learned to love both Death Valley and Walter Scott. He was an insurance executive in the Midwest who had been partially disabled in a train accident that had killed his father. In Scotty he saw the antithesis of all that was Midwestern. Scotty was the romantic ideal of the Western man, and Johnson apparently enjoyed fueling the legend. In short, Scott became Johnson's hobby.

Since I am highly recommending that you visit Scotty's Castle, I am not going to describe what you will see there or give extensive details about the

Entrance to the main residence at Death Valley Ranch

buildings themselves. The tour and available publications will do that admirably. (One brochure, "A Walking Tour of Death Valley Ranch," is particularly helpful as you stroll the grounds while you pass the time waiting for your tour to begin.) My emphasis has been on Walter Scott and the not insignificant role he had in making Death Valley the famous place it has become. Scotty would have loved that emphasis, incidentally; he was openly scornful of the attention the "castle" received, once saying, "I'm the one-man circus. The castle is just the tail of my kite."

Johnson began construction on Death Valley Ranch in 1922 in Grapevine Canyon, almost a hundred miles north of Scotty's original acreage, Camp Holdout. The first buildings were basically nothing more than large stucco boxes, but they evolved into an overall ranch design that was inspired by the architecture of Stanford University, where Johnson's wife had spent one year as a student. The buildings are lavishly appointed, yet in keeping with the desert. And several innovations, such as solar panels, make the ranch an engineering marvel for that time. Death Valley Ranch was, unfortunately, never completed. The stock-market crash and subsequent Depression caused Johnson to liquidate much of his capital and curtail construction on the project. That didn't stop Johnson and his wife, but particularly Walter Scott, from enjoying what had been completed, however.

Many evenings Scott would regale ranch guests with his tales and stories. He was, essentially, a guest himself at the ranch, but his personality and braggadocio made him the Lord of the Estate, even if he didn't own it. Death Valley Scotty told outrageous lies to an enthralled audience. One of his favorites, reported in *Desert Magazine,* was the following: "Once I found an old couple in Death Valley. They were about gone, and I only had enough water for myself, so naturally I did the only humane thing." He would wait for someone to say, "What did you do?" He would then pause for effect and finish the story: "I shot them both."

In 1941 Albert Johnson gave his rationale, as quoted in Hank Johnston's book, for his bankrolling Scotty for thirty-seven years: "I've been Scotty's gold mine all these years. Scott is a swell companion, a good camp cook, and a bear on a trail. He just likes to spend money and I like to see him spend it. . . . He's always been a wonderful companion, and that's something money can't buy. . . . Why have I staked him all these years? He repays me in laughs."

Albert Johnson died at age seventy-five in 1948 after undergoing cancer surgery. Scotty died in 1954 while being driven to a hospital in Las Vegas. He was eighty-one. What Scott wanted on his tombstone was simply "Here he is," but what was put on it reads, "I got four things to live by: Don't say nothing that will hurt anybody. Don't give advice—nobody will take it anyway. Don't complain. Don't explain." So Death Valley Scotty is a con man to the last, since every day people read that epitaph and remark on its good intent, while Walter E. Scott ignored every bit of it virtually every day of his life.

OLD STOVEPIPE WELL

Old Stovepipe Well is about 33 miles south of Scotty's Castle on the way to Stovepipe Wells Village. Take the road marked as the side trip to the sand dunes.

Stovepipe Well is not the same place as the current village. The actual well was the only water hole in the sand-dune area of Death Valley and at one time the only known water source between the boomtowns of Rhyolite, Nevada, and Skidoo (see entry, Chapter 2). Because sand sometimes obscured the site of the well, an unknown but thoughtful traveler shoved a length of stovepipe into the sand to mark the spot. Eventually a small way station grew at the site, including a store, a lodging house, and a saloon, all made of canvas. When entrepreneur Bob Eichbaum attempted to develop the commercial aspects of Death Valley as a tourist resort in 1926, he built a toll road into the Valley but had difficulty ex-

tending it across the dunes to Stovepipe Well, so he simply built his resort six miles away, and the new settlement ultimately became known by the old name.

At the site of the original well are an historic marker and the nearby grave of a Val Nolan, who was last seen alive on the Fourth of July in 1931. He was found and buried seven months later by a movie company shooting on location.

HARMONY BORAX WORKS

The Harmony Borax Works stand 1.5 miles north of the present settlement at Furnace Creek Ranch.

Despite all the frantic searching for precious minerals in Death Valley, it was the more mundane elements that brought genuine wealth to the Valley. One of those elements was borax, which has over fifty uses, including those of water softener, deodorant, shampoo, and cleanser. It has been used for centuries in such processes as pottery glazes and metal-working fluxes, and more recently in the production of fiber glass.

Aaron Winters and his wife Rosie had visitors in 1881 who showed Winters a test for borax. He immediately took his wife out to a spot in Death Valley where he had seen huge deposits of a similar substance. There he applied the test and exclaimed, "She burns green, Rosie! We're rich, by God!"

Winters sent samples to William T. Coleman in San Francisco, who paid Winters $20,000 for rights to the deposits that in 1882 became the Harmony Borax Works. Chinese workers gathered the ulexite, a fluffy-looking borax also known as "cottonball," while Indians cut wood to fuel a boiler. The cottonball was hauled in from the marshy deposits, heated in large vats in a solution of carbonate and water, and hardened to crystal form on iron rods that had been suspended in the solution. The crystals were dried, loaded on wagons pulled by eight-mule, then twelve-mule, and finally the famous twenty-mule-team wagons to Mojave, 165 miles and ten overnight stops away. Harmony Borax Works prospered until 1889, when a more profitable form of borax, named Colemanite in honor of William T. Coleman, was discovered in the mountains above the marshes, and the Old Harmony Works ceased operation.

At the site today are remnants of the old boiler, vats, and adobe walls, along with a display of twenty-mule-team wagons. Some adobe walls from

Boiler of the Harmony Borax Works; mule-team wagons on right

the company's operations stand near the road into Mustard Canyon.

When you leave the Harmony Borax Works, spend some time at Furnace Creek Ranch, the major outpost for this part of Death Valley. There you will find a visitors' center that features outstanding displays, books, and informative talks by Park Service personnel. I found the rangers to be knowledgeable, friendly, and eager to assist visitors. Don't be afraid to ask about such matters as road conditions and accommodations.

Andy Laswell, a homesteader known to legend as "Bellerin' Teck," became the first official inhabitant of Death Valley when he settled near Bennetts Well in 1870, growing hay for Panamint's Surprise Valley Mill and Water Company. He started a second hay ranch at the mouth of Furnace Creek. The creek itself had been named by Dr. Darwin French when he and three others ventured into Death Val-

ley in 1860 looking for the Gunsight Lode and found a small furnace that Asabel Bennett had constructed only weeks before to try to assay some promising ore samples. When the Harmony Borax Works began nearby, its owner, William T. Coleman, bought this neighboring property in 1883 to furnish provisions for the men and mules at the operations. The Greenland Ranch, as it was then known, was laid out and run by Rudolph Neuschwander, Coleman's superintendent. After the Harmony Borax Works shut down, the ranch was overseen by Jimmy Dayton, one of Death Valley's best-known citizens (see next entry). When the Pacific Coast Borax Company took over from Coleman, they changed the Greenland Ranch to its present name, Furnace Creek Ranch.

Today the ranch features campsites, a motel, restaurants—and all the comforts that Death Valley pioneers could not have imagined. Also at Furnace

Creek are the Furnace Creek Inn, opened in 1927 as Borax Consolidated's answer to Bob Eichbaum's Stovepipe Wells tourist attractions; an interesting borax museum; and the wonderful Old Dinah, a steam-traction train that had originally been used at Calico but was last in service for the Keane Wonder Mine (see entry, Chapter 2). It worked pretty well— on level, hard ground at three to four miles per hour. But it lost steering on hills and tended to dig itself into soft sand. Mule skinners and their teams, whom the tractor was supposed to replace, gained employment pulling Old Dinah out of trouble. It died of a ruptured boiler in November 1909 ascending Daylight Pass and remained there for two decades before being rescued to be put on display.

(*The following two sites are for the purist with a truck, and then only if the road is open*. You will be taking the West Side Road, which skirts the Devil's Golf Course and goes for 40 miles, coming back to the main road just north of the Ashford Mill ruins.)

GRAVES OF JIMMY DAYTON AND SHORTY HARRIS

The Graves of Jimmy Dayton and Shorty Harris lie about 17 miles southwest of Furnace Creek Ranch on the West Side Road.

Jimmy Dayton and Shorty Harris couldn't have been less alike, but both are famous in the history of Death Valley. Jimmy Dayton arrived in the Valley in the 1880s, working on the mule-team wagons that hauled borax to Mojave. Before the turn of the century, he became the caretaker of Greenland Ranch, later called Furnace Creek Ranch. He was well loved in the Valley, perhaps because he was so different from the mostly raucous characters who often inhabited it. A soft-spoken, down-to-earth fellow, Dayton cared for Death Valley more than he cared for anyone—even his wife. When his bride could no longer stand to live there, Jimmy sadly accompanied her out—but returned alone.

Because he was so loved, it was no small cause for alarm when a letter arrived in the Valley saying that Jimmy Dayton was overdue in Daggett, near Barstow. Adolph Nevares and Frank Tilton volunteered to look for Jimmy. They found him with the help of Dayton's emaciated, dehydrated dog, found barking in the desert. Dayton was curled up under a mesquite bush, dead, one-half mile north of the old Eagle Borax Works—and not far from where the Valley's first recorded victim, Richard Culverwell,

had died in 1850. Dayton's six mules were dead, tangled in their traces and attached to the wagon that carried their feed and water. Dayton was buried at the spot. Frank Tilton was reported to have said at the burial, "Well, Jimmy, you lived in the heat and you died in the heat, and after what you've been through, I guess you ought to be comfortable in hell." The marker, incidentally, says Dayton died in 1898, and historian W. A. Chalfant agrees; Richard Lingefelter says 1899. Dolph Nevares, who found Jimmy, claimed it happened in 1900. Lingenfelter's book shows an early photograph of Dayton's grave, covered with the bones of his mules that died near him.

Frank "Shorty" Harris was, by all accounts, a remarkable character. He had a genuine knack for finding mineral deposits and an even greater ability to ensure somehow that the real wealth went to someone else. He and Ed Cross found the deposits that led to the strikes at Bullfrog and Rhyolite, Nevada, and Shorty was with Pete Aguereberry when Pete found gold at what became Harrisburg in the Panamint Range (see Harrisburg entry, Chapter 2).

Many Death Valley denizens loved Shorty, but they also considered him to be a genial and entertaining liar and therefore a worthy subject for practical jokes. My favorite Shorty Harris tale, recounted by Lew and Ginny Clark in *High Mountains and Deep Valleys: The Gold Bonanza Days*, concerns Shorty and Ballarat. Ballarat (see entry, Chapter 2) was a Panamint Valley town known for its wild Fourth of July celebrations. One year, days after the Fourth, Shorty was in a seriously overindulged condition, passed out on the floor of Chris Wicht's saloon. The boys in the bar decided to pull one on Shorty, so they lifted him into a pine box, placed a sheet over his body, with only his face showing, and put the box, surrounded by lighted candles, onto Wicht's pool table. When Shorty finally came around, he overheard conversations about what a nice fellow he'd been and how they hoped he'd found that great gold mine in the sky. They then blew out the candles, picked up the coffin, and headed out to the cemetery. Shorty started screaming. He didn't show up again in Ballarat for some time.

But Shorty Harris did finally return to Ballarat. In fact, he was the only person living in the ghost town before he was taken to Lone Pine, where he died in 1934. He is buried, however, not in the Ballarat or Lone Pine cemeteries, but next to his friend Jimmy Dayton. The grave marker tells it all:

SHORTY HARRIS (1856–1934)
BURY ME BESIDE JIM DAYTON IN THE VALLEY
WE LOVED. ABOVE ME WRITE, "HERE LIES
SHORTY HARRIS, A SINGLE BLANKET JACKASS
PROSPECTOR."

EAGLE BORAX WORKS

*The Eagle Borax Works ruins stand south of Day-
ton's and Harris's graves. A sign leads you to
the site.*

Isadore Daunet, a Frenchman, first saw borax deposits when he traversed Death Valley in 1880 but did
not know their value. When he heard of Aaron Winters' discovery in 1881, he and two partners—Jim
McDonald and C. C. Blanch—returned to Death
Valley in May 1882. Theirs were the first borax
works in the Valley, but the efforts lasted only two
years and had a total production of only 130 tons
because of eventual competition from the Harmony
Works and severe transportation problems. Daunet,
who lost all his money and eventually his wife,

Ruins of vat of the Eagle Borax Works

All that remains of the Eagle Borax Works boiler

Concrete foundations of the Ashford Mill

killed himself with a single bullet in May 1884. All
that remain today of the Eagle Borax Works are
stone foundations and sparse ruins of the iron boiler
and a vat.

ASHFORD MILL

*The Ashford Mill ruins are about 45 miles south of
Furnace Creek Ranch and about 2 miles south of
the junction with the West Side Road.*

The Ashford brothers—Henry, Harold, and
Louis—found and worked the Golden Treasure
Mine starting in 1907. Their mill, now in ruins on
the west side of the highway, was constructed in
1914, when the Ashfords' mine and the nearby Carbonate Mine were operating. The Ashford brothers
sold their claim to a self-styled Hungarian noble-
man for $60,000, who in turn sold it for $105,000
to Benjamin McCausland and his son. The latter apparently were unable to make the claims pay. One
story says the cement company that sent material
for the construction of the mill accidentally sent a
double order, which accounts for the thickness of
the walls. Despite its sturdiness, however, the mill
was inefficient and was abandoned after only a few
tons had been milled.

Area Two: The Eastern
Ranges

LEADFIELD

*Leadfield is 16 miles from state route 374 on the
road through Titus Canyon. You reach the turnoff
to Titus Canyon by driving into Nevada at a point*

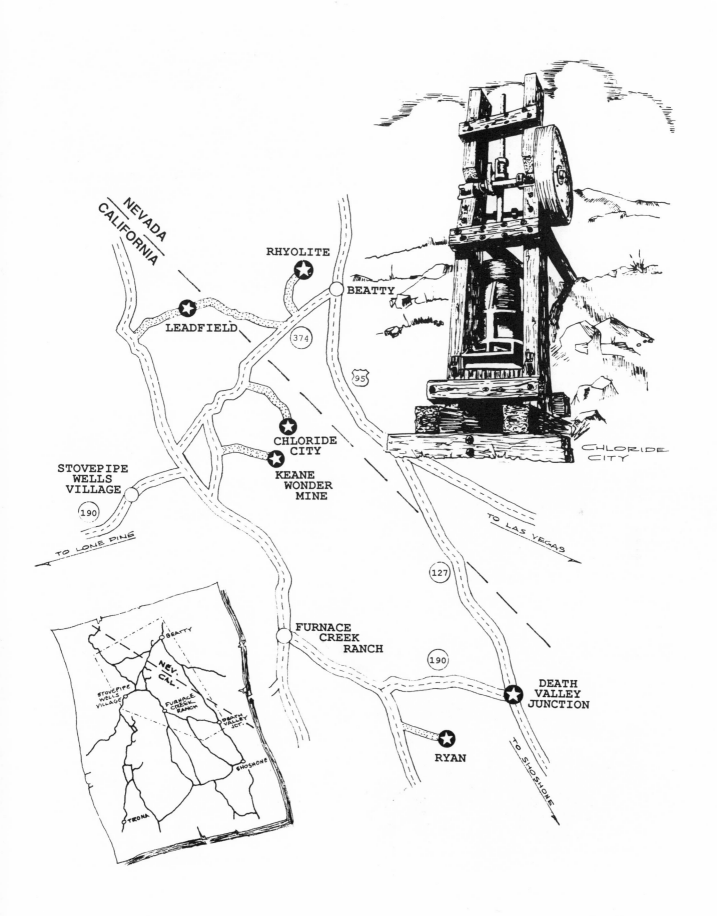

NEVADA
CALIFORNIA

RHYOLITE ⭐

BEATTY

LEADFIELD ⭐

374

95

CHLORIDE
CITY

CHLORIDE ⭐
CITY

KEANE
WONDER
MINE

STOVEPIPE
WELLS
VILLAGE

190

TO LONE PINE

TO LAS VEGAS

127

FURNACE
CREEK
RANCH

190

DEATH ⭐
VALLEY
JUNCTION

RYAN ⭐

TO SHOSHONE

BEATTY

NEV.
CAL.

STOVEPIPE
WELLS
VILLAGE

FURNACE
CREEK
RANCH

DEATH
VALLEY
JCT.

SHOSHONE

TRONA

about 6 miles west of Beatty. While you're this close, go investigate the Nevada ghost towns of Rhyolite and Bullfrog. (As they are in Nevada, not California, this book will not tell their stories. But Lingenfelter has an excellent chapter on the area [pp. 203–41], and Stanley Paher's Nevada Ghost Towns and Mining Camps *and his* Death Valley Ghost Towns *have histories and photographs.) The road to Leadfield is one way for most of the route, including the section through the townsite. This is definitely a truck road because of steep grades and sand. The park service recommends four-wheel drive. The total distance from state route 374 to state route 190 in Death Valley is 28 miles.*

If the road is open and your vehicle is capable, this is a must-see trip. The drive to Leadfield is spectacular—varied colors, rock formations, geologic upheavals, dramatic vistas—and the site itself is in a magnificent canyon in the Grapevine Mountains. The drive from Leadfield to Death Valley is even better, as it passes through the narrow cliffs of Titus Canyon, named for Morris Titus, a young mining engineer who left the canyon while searching for water for himself and two friends and died on the Valley floor. At some points in Titus Canyon your truck almost seems to touch the walls on either side. It is unforgettable. The 16 miles to Leadfield will take you about an hour. The journey from the townsite to the floor of Death Valley, 12 miles, will require about forty minutes.

Leadfield itself features three corrugated buildings under roof, one a false front; a miner's rock dugout; and a couple of adits and waste dumps. The reason for the rather skimpy remains is simple; Leadfield was far more impressive on paper and in the descriptions by the promoter than it ever was in real life. Or, as W. A. Chalfant wryly reports, Lead-

Dumps from the worthless mines at Leadfield and two of the three remaining buildings

field had all the qualities of a successful mining camp except paying ore.

Charles Courtney Julian knew how to promote a loser. He had been suspected of an oil swindle in Southern California with his Julian Petroleum Company, known as "Julian Pete," which Julian claimed would "make that Standard Oil crowd turn flip-flops." In May of 1926 he was beginning to suck in investors with the opportunity of Western Lead, named for the spectacular lead deposits he claimed were just waiting to be tapped in the Grapevine Mountains. Pockets of investors were what were about to be tapped. One account says that Julian had lead hauled in from Tonopah to salt the canyon. Chalfant states that Julian took out full-page ads in newspapers offering tours and other incentives to would-be investors; Ruth Kirk, in *Exploring Death Valley,* claims that Julian distributed handbills showing lead-laden steamers negotiating the flowing Amargosa River. That is chutzpah. When you're in Beatty, be sure to notice the flowing Amargosa. Julian next rented a train, filled with 340 "lucky" investors, which went from Los Angeles to Beatty, Nevada, at which point the group was escorted into ninety waiting automobiles and driven to the site of the excitement along with over 800 others who provided their own transportation.

About 300 people believed sufficiently in Julian's claims to come live in Leadfield, and many more were absentee investors. The townsfolk, naturally, found out in fairly short order that the place was a

Corrugated building at Leadfield

scam, and Leadfield was dead eight months after it was born. Arthur R. Benton, in an article in *Desert Magazine*, reported how he and a friend drove a Model T Ford up the wrong way on the one-way road through Titus Canyon to Leadfield in an erroneous search for Scotty's Castle, then under construction. He noted that the men in Leadfield were in a rather ugly mood. Later he found out that they had been bilked and were apparently beginning to realize it.

Julian made a reported $900,000 on his Leadfield swindle and successfully pulled off scams in Arizona and Oklahoma before being forced to bolt to Shanghai in 1933 to avoid prosecution. There, penniless, he committed suicide in 1934. If C. C. Julian had only promoted the spot for its scenery and healthful climate, Leadfield might be alive today.

Miner's stone dugout at Chloride City

Auto body at Chloride City. The floor of Death Valley is in the background, with the Panamint Range towering over it.

CHLORIDE CITY

A large sign stands on state route 374 between Beatty, Nevada, and Death Valley on the north side of the road marking your entrance into the national monument. Across the highway at this point, a dirt road heads south. It is the best road to Chloride City. Follow it for almost 7 miles, take the right fork, and proceed up into the Funeral Mountains for another 4 miles. Here take the left fork. To this point a passenger car would have little difficulty. From here the road will become appreciably steeper, but the townsite is only about a mile away. A truck can continue easily.

Hikers I met at the Keane Wonder Mine who had come down from the Chloride Cliff Mine assured

Chloride Cliff Mine's one-stamp mill that reportedly worked for only one day

Stamp mill at Chloride Cliff Mine overlooks the floor of Death Valley, with the Panamint Mountains in the background.

me that nothing worth looking at remained at Chloride City. Well, "nothing" in this case is plenty. When you top the hill that overlooks the main townsite, you will see, to the south, mill foundations with a water tank, a wooden floor on a stone foundation, the rusted bodies of a car and truck (probably dating from the late '20s), and a roofed shack on a rise beyond the townsite. You will also have a startlingly magnificent view of the Panamint Mountains and the Sierra Nevadas.

After examining the townsite, go up to the miner's shack on the hill. The back wall leads into an adit, so use caution. Next to the building is a grave.

Now proceed up the hill to the south. When you reach the crest, you'll see a corrugated tin building and, down in the wash, a series of three stone buildings in varying states of decline.

But the best is ahead: drive through the wash and up the steep hill to the south. Your goal is the barbed-wire fence that surrounds a shaft on the top of the hill. Park your truck by this fenced-in shaft.

Two roads branch off at this point. Unless you have four-wheel drive, I'd recommend leaving your vehicle here, because both branches in the road become rather steep and narrow. The right fork terminates in .3 miles at one of the most memorable overlooks in Death Valley. The road actually continues down toward the Keane Wonder Mine, but it is closed to vehicles. The left fork in the road winds along the mountain's edge to the Chloride Cliff Mine, where you will find a hopper and a tunnel. From that point, look down the ravine. There, about 1,000 feet below, is a perfect example of a one-stamp mill which, according to Death Valley Park Ranger Bill Schreier, was operated for only one day. I have never seen a mill in as excellent condition as this one. I suggest you go down one of two ways. The faster is to slide and shuffle down the ravine as best you can. The easier but longer route begins right where you left your vehicle, at the fenced-in shaft.

Chloride City was the living quarters for the

Chloride Cliff Mine. Deposits were found there in 1871, much earlier than most of the other discoveries in the eastern part of Death Valley. But the deposits were lead chloride, not silver chloride as the prospectors had hoped, and the mine never really paid. W. A. Chalfant reports that the camp once featured a bunkhouse, cookhouse, blacksmith shop, assay office, and the mine superintendent's house. Water was pumped in about four miles from Keane Springs, and it was such a precious commodity that a watchman was assigned to walk the route looking for leaks.

Although the first mining efforts lasted only a few years, one important consequence of the ore's discovery was the construction of the first road across Death Valley, through Wingate Wash, and on to Barstow, thereby opening up the Valley to transportation from the south and west. Mining efforts were undertaken again in 1916, but they lasted only about two years. Most remnants at Chloride City probably date from this later occupation.

Four tram support towers along the Keane Wonder Mine tramway.

KEANE WONDER MINE

The road to the Keane Wonder Mine is clearly marked at a spot 5.6 miles north of the turnoff to Beatty from Furnace Creek Ranch. This good dirt road proceeds 2.7 miles to a parking area below the mine. The total distance from Stovepipe Wells Village is 22 miles.

In 1904 an Irishman, Jack Keane, and his partner, Domingo Etcharren, were looking for silver but discovered gold on the western slope of the Funeral Mountains. They developed their claim into the Keane Wonder Mine, but both eventually sold their interest in the claims for $50,000 in cash and a considerable amount of stock. With his money, Etcharren bought a store in Darwin. Keane's story isn't as happy; he returned to Ireland, committed murder, and was sentenced to seventeen years in prison.

The Keane Wonder Gold Mining Company began operations in 1904, and the original work lasted until 1912. It was opened again in the 1930s, and most of the remains at the site today are from that

Lower tram terminus at the Keane Wonder Mine

Ruins of the upper tram terminus of the Keane Wonder Mine in the Funeral Mountains

later attempt. Estimates of the total gold and silver production for the mine vary from between $750,000 to $1 million.

At the end of a short walk from your car are a tram terminus, mill foundations, a chute, water tanks, and a park-service sign explaining the Keane Wonder Mine. If you are a good walker, be sure to follow the trail to the mine itself. The view from Chloride City, less than two air miles from the mine, is more spectacular, perhaps, because Chloride City sits at twice the 2500-foot elevation of Keane Wonder Mine. But somehow the view can be better appreciated at the mine after the one-hour climb on a clearly marked trail that follows the water line and the old tramway towers from the mill site up to the mine ruins. There you will find extensive tunneling, the tramway platform, water tanks, buckets, ore cars, and foundations. The tramway, known as the "sky railroad," was gravity powered,

Looking from the upper tram terminus at Keane Wonder Mine down to the floor of Death Valley

with the descending buckets, full of ore, lifting the ascending buckets, which carried supplies and even passengers up nearly a mile to the mine site.

Plan to spend about an hour prowling the area at the end of your hike. I explored Keane Wonder Mine in an afternoon in December, and nothing of that visit to Death Valley was as beautiful as watching the shadows lengthen over the Valley as the sun dropped down behind the Panamint Range.

RYAN

The road to Ryan is 14.6 miles southeast of Furnace Creek Ranch. Take the turnoff from state route 190 that heads toward Dantes View; Ryan will become visible up on the side of the Greenwater Mountains to your left.

Most ghost towns and mines featured so far in this chapter have been principally "precious metals" sites, but as mentioned in the Harmony Borax Works

entry, more wealth was mined from Death Valley for a longer period of time from less exciting minerals. A case in point are the two sites that have been called Ryan, worked for borax since before the turn of the century. Nothing except tailings remain at the original Ryan, which was southwest of Death Valley Junction. The Pacific Coast Borax Company began operations there at the Lila C. Mine in 1890; principal production occurred from 1907 until 1914. The Lila C. produced over $8 million in colemanite borax, making it richer than all the other Death Valley mines combined.

When the Lila C. apparently played out in 1914, Pacific Coast Borax relocated its headquarters at Devair (or Devar), but they took along the name of Ryan (in honor of John Ryan, for many years the manager of the company) to the Devair townsite. There they erected a model company town of family homes, a bunkhouse, a school, a combination

The considerable remains of "New" Ryan as seen from the "no trespassing" sign

Photograph of Ryan taken with a 205mm lens—old church from Rhyolite is clearly visible at left; former dormitories, later the Death Valley View Hotel, are in foreground.

movie theater and recreation hall (the Catholic church building moved from Rhyolite), and even tennis courts. They began shipping borax from the "new" Ryan in 1915. The principal mines were the Louise, the Grand View, the Oakley, the Widow, and the Upper and Lower Biddies. The Lila C., moreover, was not finished yet; it was reopened in 1920 after new deposits were found there while workmen were tearing up its abandoned trackage. The Lila C. closed for good in 1927.

The population of the new Ryan probably peaked at about 250. Ryan's deposits became unprofitable in 1927 with the discovery of more easily mined borax at the new site of Boron in the Mojave Desert. The most profitable mining venture in Death Valley history had ended, but not before over $30 million in borax had been shipped. The post office closed down in 1930, and Ryan became a ghost, except on occasion when Ryan's former dormitory, converted to the Death Valley View Hotel, was opened occasionally to accommodate overflow guests from Furnace Creek. In the 1930s, a seven-mile stretch of the narrow-gauge railroad was in operation for tourists at the cost of one dollar per person.

A sign on the road to Ryan establishes that Ryan is not open to the public. Park Ranger Bill Schreier told me that you will be firmly denied access to Ryan if you ignore the warning sign. But from the road, with binoculars or a telescope, you can still get a fairly good view of the town. Eight buildings, three of which have two stories, are visible. You can also make out an ore car and various other pieces of mine equipment.

DEATH VALLEY JUNCTION

Death Valley Junction is 27 miles north of Shoshone on state route 127 and 29 miles southeast of Furnace Creek Ranch on state route 190.

Despite its name, Death Valley Junction is not in Death Valley. In fact, it is vastly different in appearance from the other ghost towns in this chapter. This is a desert plains town; at over 2,000 feet, it is far higher than the ghosts of the Valley floor but much lower than mountain sites like Panamint or Chloride City. Nor is it nestled near dramatic mountains, like Ballarat and Ryan.

Death Valley Junction came into being because it was here that the Tonopah and Tidewater Rail-

Commercial building at Death Valley Junction

road—completed between Ludlow and Beatty (Nevada) in 1907—connected to a branch line out to the borax deposits of the Pacific Coast Borax Company's Lila C. Mine. (For more on the Tonopah and Tidewater, see the Ludlow entry; for more on the Lila C., see Ryan, the previous entry.) Death Valley Junction stood 47 miles south of Beatty and 122 miles north of Ludlow along the "T & T."

In 1914, when Pacific Coast Borax moved its operations to "new" Ryan, the Death Valley Railroad was incorporated and a narrow-gauge line was extended on to the new borax mine and company headquarters from a point along the old rail route between Death Valley Junction and the Lila C. Mine. Because it was a narrow-gauge line, a third rail had to be inserted between the existing rails back to the Tonopah and Tidewater at Death Valley Junction. A 1915 map of the Junction shows the narrow- and regular-gauge rail lines, a depot, a water tank, the shops of the Death Valley Railroad, eight houses, a store, a cafe, and a saloon.

That 1915 map shows Death Valley Junction at the beginning of its peak years; a mill was built there to handle the increased production of the Ryan borax mines, since its output was double that of the Lila C. Mine. By 1919 the mill was running twenty-four hours a day.

Pacific Coast Borax began some significant improvements to Death Valley Junction in 1923, at least partly in response to disparaging remarks made by visitor Zane Grey, who embarrassed the company and the town in an article published in *Harper's Magazine*. Pacific Coast Borax built a Civic Center—completed in 1924 at a cost of $300,000—that featured their company offices, employee sleeping quarters, and such refinements as a gymnasium, a billiard room, an ice-cream parlor, and a meeting hall-theater known as Corkhill Hall. In 1927, the year the Ryan operation closed down, the Civic Center was remodeled to become the Amargosa Hotel as part of an effort to entice tourists to Death Valley.

The Tonopah and Tidewater moved its shops from Ludlow to Death Valley Junction in the 1930s as an economy move, and the cutback was a sign of worse things to come. The rails were torn up from Beatty to Ludlow between the summers of 1942 and '43; many of the ties were used to build the El Rancho Motel in Barstow. Death Valley Junction was no longer a junction at all.

Today this desert ghost town consists of an inter-

Death Valley Junction's cemetery; in the background is the southernmost part of the Funeral Mountains.

esting, barren cemetery on the south end of town, a large commercial building on the tracks side of town, and, across the highway, the closed Amargosa Hotel. Corkhill Hall is now the Amargosa Opera House, where Marta Beckett, a professional dancer formerly of New York, performs a unique one-person show.

Area Three: The Panamint Range

SKIDOO

Skidoo is 27 miles from Stovepipe Wells Village. About 10.5 miles south of the junction of state route 190 and the road through Emigrant Canyon, turn east at the monument sign pointing the way. The townsite is 8 miles up a dirt road that is a little rough, but a passenger car should make it without difficulty.

In January 1906 John L. Ramsey and John "One-Eye" Thompson found a large primary deposit they called the Gold Eagle, a strike so large that it required thirty claims to cover it. Rhyolite mining tycoon Bob Montgomery bought out Ramsey and Thompson for $30,000 each. Montgomery then sank $200,000 into twenty-one miles of eight-inch iron pipe brought in from the railhead at Johannesburg (see entry, Chapter 3) to construct a pipeline to the townsite from Birch Spring on Telescope Peak—the highest point in the Panamint Range. The pipe's purpose was to supply water to run a fifteen-stamp mill, which began operation in 1907.

Several stories explain the naming of the town,

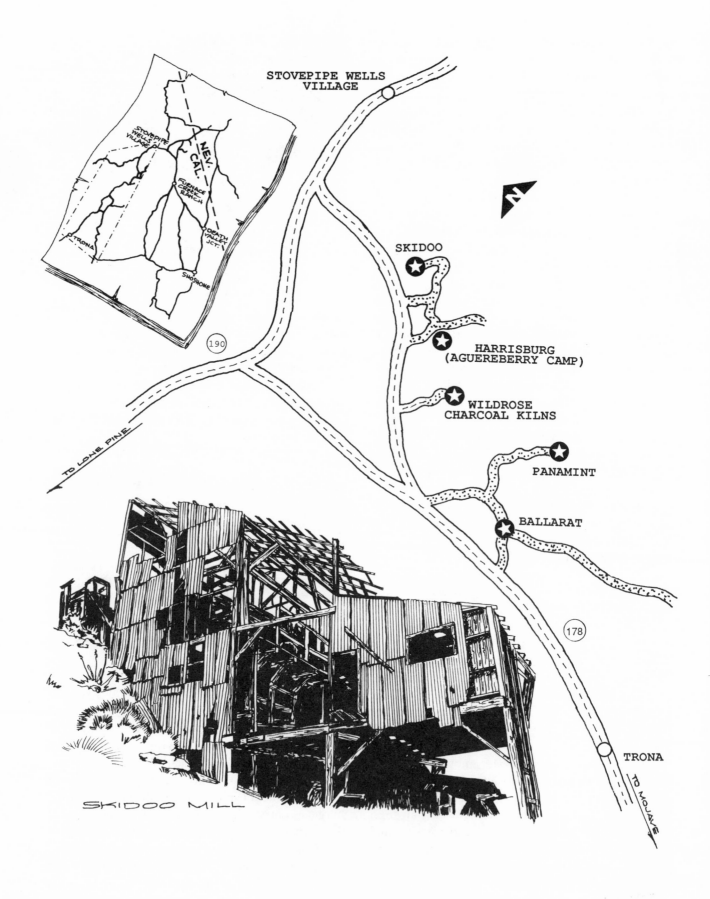

STOVEPIPE WELLS
VILLAGE

NEV.
CAL.

STOVEPIPE
WELLS
VILLAGE

FURNACE
CREEK
RANCH

DEATH
VALLEY
JCT.

TRONA

SHOSHONE

(190)

TO LONE PINE

SKIDOO

HARRISBURG
(AGUEREBERRY CAMP)

WILDROSE
CHARCOAL KILNS

PANAMINT

BALLARAT

(178)

TRONA

TO MOJAVE

SKIDOO MILL

but Richard Lingenfelter says that the name simply came about because Bob Montgomery's wife Winnie, hearing that her husband had bought twenty-three claims, said, "23 Skidoo," which was a popular slang expression meaning "skeedaddle"—"let's get out of here fast." Lingenfelter adds that Montgomery wanted the town named after himself. The U.S. Post Office rejected that name, as it was already in use. They rejected Skidoo out of hand as unacceptably frivolous, choosing "Hoveck" instead, in honor of mine general manager Matt Hoveck. However, popular sentiment prevailed and Bob Montgomery and the post office capitulated. Skidoo became official on April 1, 1907—April Fool's Day.

Many of the miners who settled the one-owner company town were, like Montgomery, from Rhyolite, and telephone and telegraph lines connected the two sites. Skidoo featured the usual mining town establishments with a couple of refinements. It had its own newspaper, the *Skidoo News,* and the Tucki Club, organized by Montgomery and Hoveck,

a members-only club with elegant rooms and fare. Because Skidoo was under the fairly strong hand of one person, it was considered a rather quiet, even uneventful place to live.

Yet the most famous story of Skidoo is hardly quiet and uneventful. In April 1908 one of the town's least popular fellows, Joe L. "Hootch" Simpson, shot and killed one of the most popular, Jim Arnold, who had earlier kicked the drunken and surly Simpson. Simpson, according to the town doctor, might have had syphilis and was under the influence of narcotics. Those possibly extenuating circumstances did not deter an angry mob, which took Simpson from the sheriff and summarily hanged him from a telephone pole. The *Skidoo News,* reveling in the frontier justice, said that would-be outlaws should ". . . note the number, the stoutness, and the great convenience of the telephone poles, and reflect thereon."

The morning after the hanging, Dr. Reginald Macdonald took two photographs of Simpson's corpse, one on the table and one hanging from a

The dramatic Skidoo Mill; note the wooden belt wheel at the center of the photograph.

The Skidoo Mill; the fifteen stamps are visible in the center of this photo.

beam in the tent that served as a makeshift morgue. That photograph is reproduced in Lingenfelter's book and in George Pipkin's book on Pete Aguereberry (see Bibliography). Lingenfelter says further that the body was first dumped down a mine shaft, then brought up by Dr. Macdonald, who beheaded the corpse to examine the brain for signs of syphilis. He kept the skull, and it has been passed from one person to another over the years. According to W. A. Chalfant, in his book *The Story of Inyo,* the noose used in the original hanging was treasured by a "morbid-minded" bartender.

The population of Skidoo may have reached 700, and the post office was open from 1907 until 1917, when Montgomery's mine closed after having produced $1.34 million in gold. The pipeline was taken up and sold for scrap, and the last gold-mining camp in Death Valley was dead.

Skidoo doesn't look particularly promising at first glance. No buildings stand at the townsite, and only a national monument sign lets you know that you have arrived. Some rusty cans and broken glass lie nearby, and there is no indication that anything else

of interest is left. But there is. From the Skidoo sign, follow the right fork of the road until, in .6 miles, there is another fork. Here go left for .3 miles and park your vehicle next to an adit. After a short walk, one of Death Valley's most surprising and dramatic sights will appear around the bend: the fifteen-stamp Skidoo mill. All its stamps are there, and the mill itself perches on a steep ravine that provides one of the Valley's best photographic locations. Warning: Be careful around the old mill, as it is rather rickety. And please leave it as you found it—one of the West's most picturesque buildings.

HARRISBURG/AGUEREBERRY CAMP

From the turnoff to Skidoo, head south 2.4 miles and take the road marked as the way to Aguereberry Point. Continue on this road for 1.5 miles and take the fork to the right that leads up to the group of white buildings.

On July 1, 1905, Pete Aguereberry and his trail partner Shorty Harris, recent acquaintances who

The boarded-up buildings of Pete Aguereberry's headquarters; the hole in the wall on the right side of the main residence afforded the view of Pete's kitchen (see photo below).

were traveling together as a safety precaution common in Death Valley, were journeying to the Fourth of July celebration in Ballarat. That was the place to be for the Fourth in Death Valley (see Shorty Harris entry, Chapter 2, for the account of another Ballarat Fourth of July blowout that Shorty attended). On what is now known as Harrisburg Flats, Pete found an outcropping of gold and showed it to Shorty. Pete staked claims for each of them while Shorty went after burros that had strayed. Harris's desire to share the news, despite Aguereberry's pleas for secrecy, led to a horde of about 300 prospectors combing the area by September.

Originally the camp that formed there was to be called Harrisberry, honoring both discoverers, but Shorty called it Harrisburg, which riled Pete. The actual town never amounted to much more than a single saloon and a general store. More substantial deposits found five months later at nearby Skidoo soon caused an exodus from Harrisburg. Years after both camps were ghost towns, Pete Aguereberry returned to the original claim and provided a modest living for himself, although more from grubstakes and odd jobs than from paying ore.

Jean Pierre "Pete" Aguereberry was a Basque immigrant who became a sheepherder in California, as did many of his countrymen. He tired of that

life and next became a prospector, attracted by the strikes at Goldfield, Rhyolite, and Bullfrog. Pete's experiences are a testimony to the difficulties of attempting to scratch out a living in Death Valley. First there were disagreements with Shorty Harris about who had claims at the site. Later, Pete had recurring legal problems trying to establish sole claim

Pete Aguereberry's kitchen

Wooden ore chute at Pete Aguereberry's diggings

to his properties. And on Easter Sunday, 1939, a ton and a half of Pete's hand-picked, best high-grade ore was hijacked while Pete attended church services.

Pete's health suffered as well; he contracted silicosis, a lung disease often caught by miners from breathing mine dust and which miners ominously called "rocks in the box." Pete Aguereberry died in 1945 at age seventy-two. He was found floating facedown in the hot springs at Tecopa, California, and is buried at the Mount Whitney Cemetery in Lone Pine. George Pipkin, a friend of Aguereberry's for twenty years, describes Pete's life in detail in the informative and interesting *Pete Aguereberry: Death Valley Prospector and Gold Miner* (see Bibliography).

The buildings and diggings that comprise Harrisburg now are actually Aguereberry Camp, as they are the remains of Pete's efforts. Three small shacks, one shed, and an outhouse cluster together

on the north side of a hill, and through the windows you can see tables, chairs, kitchen appliances, and foodstuffs, reminders of where Pete lived for forty years. Signs are prominently posted reminding you that the area is property of the U.S. Government, and you are warned to leave the buildings alone. Unfortunately, there is ample evidence that some have not heeded the admonition. A short distance away from the camp is an ore chute and the bullet-riddled body of a '40s-era Buick. On the other side of the hill is the mine that Aguereberry worked.

Bob Eichbaum, the entrepreneur of Stovepipe Wells Village, in an attempt to lure tourists his way (and away from the increasingly popular eastern floor spots like Furnace Creek and Dante's View), extended a road in the winter of 1929 from Harrisburg Flats to a spot he called Grand View, now known as Aguereberry Point. From there you can see the highest and lowest points, Mount Whitney and Badwater, in the contiguous states.

WILDROSE CHARCOAL KILNS

From the turnoff to Harrisburg and Aguereberry Point, head south on the road through Emigrant Canyon to the turnoff at the Wildrose Ranger Station and Campground. The seven-mile road to the charcoal kilns is paved for all but the last part. The total distance from Stovepipe Wells Village to the Wildrose turnoff is about 29 miles.

Some places fail to live up to their expectations, and a writer can only hope that his readers will share his enthusiasm for his favorites. He also knows that often his personal preferences will not be the same as those of his readers. But it is difficult to imagine that anyone who has an interest in the history of the West would be anything less than awed by the charcoal kilns near Wildrose Spring. Ten rock "beehive" kilns, averaging just over twenty-five feet tall and thirty feet in diameter, stand like an honor guard at the mouth of Wildrose Canyon.

I confess to being nearly a kiln fanatic. I have walked for hours in New Mexico to view the remarkable brick Catskill kilns, and I have been foolish enough to cross the Gila River in Arizona on an air mattress to get a closeup look at the Cochran kilns. Well, the Wildrose kilns are the most accessible of the three, and they rival the others for beauty. You can drive right up to these in a passenger car,

and what that takes away in challenge it certainly makes up for in convenience.

The discovery of lead ore on the western side of the Panamint Valley in 1875 at the Modoc Mine (original spelling—Modock) created a need for a smelter there, but that particular area has a notable lack of wood for fuel. The solution was found 25 miles away across the valley, up in the Panamints, at an altitude of about 7,000 feet. There these kilns, designed by Swiss engineers, were constructed by Chinese laborers in 1877 to convert piñon pine logs into charcoal through a slow, controlled burning process.

From the kilns, look across Panamint Valley to the mountains on the other side. If you cross the valley to the area of Lookout Mountain, you will see, on the Minietta Mine Road, the still-active Modoc Mine, closed to visitors, and the Minietta Mine, which has a couple of remains at the base of Lookout Mountain (also posted against trespassing but clearly visible through binoculars). Author Remi Nadeau, whose great-great-grandfather drove his mule teams laden with charcoal from Wildrose to the smelters at the Modoc and Minietta mines, says that foundations of several buildings still stand at Lookout, the old mining camp high above the mines.

An excellent source for detailed information on

Nine of the ten beehive kilns in Wildrose Canyon

Wildrose kilns—wood was loaded in these upper portals and then burned at a slow, controlled heat to make charcoal.

the kilns and the overall operation, available at various places in the national monument, is the pamphlet "Wildrose Charcoal Kilns" by Robert J. Murphy, former superintendent of Death Valley National Monument.

PANAMINT

From Wildrose Canyon, head south to the junction with the road going south from state route 190. The first dirt road bearing east after that junction is Indian Ranch Road. Follow that road for several miles until you can see a road coming down from an alluvial fan in the mountains to your left. That is the road to Panamint, and it joins Indian Ranch Road at a spot where a large boulder sits in the "Y" of the dirt road on your left. Turn there and proceed up the canyon. (The directions from Ballarat are much simpler—that same turnoff to Panamint is 2 miles north of Ballarat.) The distance to Panamint from this turnoff is just over 9 miles.

The road to Panamint (aka Panamint City) is a Jekyll and Hyde. For the first four miles it is tame and beautiful as you drive up the alluvial fan at the mouth of Surprise Canyon to a place known as Chris Wicht Camp. Wicht rented cabins at this camp in the 1930s for $1 per night; he built a seventy-five-foot pool there "big enough so a frog could get a swim." He also owned a saloon in Ballarat (see Shorty Harris and Ballarat entries, Chapter 2). From Chris Wicht Camp the road becomes treacherous and steep (up to thirty-percent grades), and only four-wheel drive vehicles or sand buggies should attempt to go past this point. The remaining five miles of the journey, which will take you up almost four thousand feet, will be eventful and slow—

but well worth it. You'll crawl through narrow canyons, cross streams several times, and observe some of the most spectacular scenery that the Death Valley area has to offer.

You'll know you're nearing Panamint when you start to see rock foundations along the canyon, then rock walls, and finally the most impressive sight of all—the brick stack of the stamp mill standing regally at the townsite. The Wyoming Mine, above the stack, has been worked in the 1980s, but I was received pleasantly enough when I established that I wanted only to look at the ghostly remains and not interfere with the work in progress.

The most dramatic ruins, certainly, are of the old twenty-stamp mill. A historical photograph of the operation is on page 41 of Paher's *Death Valley*

The brick stack of the Panamint Mill

Ruins of the Panamint Mill

Ghost Towns. Many rock walls, including a mule corral, are evident on the north side of the canyon. Behind the walls, in a cave in the canyon, are some well-preserved pictographs, perhaps done by the Shoshone, who roamed the Panamints before the arrival of miners. A less imaginative addition to a wall in the Lewis shaft above town recalls a notorious inhabitant: Charles Manson's name was inscribed there in the 1960s, a reminder that he and his followers once lived in the deserted mine buildings.

"Surprise" is the name of the canyon, and at least three versions exist to account for the naming of the place. First, it could have been named for the unexpected discovery of ore in 1873. Or, the name could have preceded that discovery. One source claims that in 1861 Dr. Samuel George, in search of the Lost Gunsight Lode (see Darwin entry, Chapter 1), was suspicious of his guide, Indian George, and would proceed no farther than a mile into the canyon, fearing a surprise attack. A third version says that thieves were using the canyon because it made an excellent fortress; anyone trying to enter the canyon would be readily observed and would make an easy target. Surprise!

In the spring of 1873 Richard Jacobs and two partners made a silver chloride find they called the Wonder of the World, with an estimated value of as much as $3,000 per ton. This brought about the creation of the Panamint Mining District. By October of the next year, an estimated 400 people were in the camp, and a year later the population had exploded to as many as 2,000 optimists. The two U.S. Senators from Nevada, John P. Jones and William Morris Stewart, invested over $250,000 in buying up many of the original claims and formed the Surprise Valley Mill and Water Company. Both had made considerable fortunes in the Comstock Lode and were known as the "Silver Senators." The fact that they were backing Panamint's boom added to the legitimacy of the camp.

The main street was a mile long and featured about 200 houses, a hotel, over two dozen saloons, a brewery, the office of the Panamint *News*, the Bank of Panamint, and even a meat market, the wagon for which also doubled as the town hearse. In Little Chief Canyon behind Main Street were the cribs of Martha Camp's brothel. Three stage lines ran almost daily service to Los Angeles, Lone Pine, and Bakersfield, the latter two making connections to places like San Francisco and Virginia City.

Panamint was known as one of the roughest, most lawless places in the West, with about fifty fatal shootings during its short life. Because of the constant threat of robbery, silver was cast into ingots weighing over 400 pounds (worth about $6,200 each) so no one could carry them off. Wells Fargo superintendent John Valentine called the place a "suburb of hell."

The suburb of hell lasted only three years. The veins played out, capital dried up as stocks fell because of an oversell swindle, and the mill was silent by 1876. Legend says that a rain squall in July of that year dumped enough water above town to cause a torrent that rushed through Surprise Canyon, knocking down stone walls and shacks and damaging the mill, but Richard Lingenfelter insists that the storm missed Surprise Canyon. He does say, however, that a flood in the summer of 1901 came through the canyon, washing out many abandoned buildings in the dead camp. The huge Panamint mill, the most dramatic ruin at the site today, burned in 1883, perhaps by arson as part of a scheme to bilk investors and an insurance company as the final act of an "on-paper-only" plan to reopen the Panamint claims.

BALLARAT

Ballarat is 2 miles south of the turnoff to Panamint, or, coming from the south, about 26 miles northeast of Trona.

Ballarat stands at the dusty foot of the Panamint Range, only about seven air miles from Panamint

Ballarat—poured adobe building

City, but 5,000 feet below it and seemingly a world away. This is a desert ghost, the first site I visited on my initial trip to Death Valley. It was about what I had expected to be the typical Death Valley ghost town. On that point I was absolutely wrong; most sites are up in the mountains, off the valley floor.

Four adobe buildings under roof, several foundations, some partial buildings, a couple of newer structures, and a cemetery comprise Ballarat. The adobe buildings are not made of the usual adobe block, but rather are adobe monoliths, according to writer-historian Paul B. Hubbard. Adobe was mixed with cement and water and poured into forms about three feet high. After the sun dried the first level, the frames were used to pour the second.

Ballarat was founded in the late 1890s and became the chief supply station for the mines on both sides of the Panamint Valley. The name was suggested by Australian George Riggins in hopeful emulation of the Australian gold-mining district that had produced some remarkable nuggets in the 1850s. The district's biggest producing mine was Henry C. Ratcliff's Never Give Up claim, later known simply as the Ratcliff, which began production in May 1896. Another winner was George and Bob Montgomery's World Beater Mine, which started up four months later.

The biggest years were from 1897 to 1902, when Ballarat featured a post office, a jail, a school, seven saloons, a Wells Fargo station, and no church, but three hotels, including the two-story Ballarat Hotel, owned by Mr. and Mrs. John Calloway. The downstairs of the hotel was adobe and contained a saloon, lobby, dining room, kitchen, and living quarters. The second floor, made of wood, had twelve rooms and a veranda. Despite this elaborate elegance, Mel Stanford, writing about Ballarat as a visitor in 1904, dryly remarked, "I wasn't overly impressed by what I saw."

By 1900, the Ballarat area featured seven working mills with a total of about sixty stamps. But in 1901 Ballarat prospectors emptied the town in favor of the enormous strikes in Tonopah, Nevada. A second attempt at the World Beater and other mines kept Ballarat alive from 1902 to 1905. Bob Montgomery, partner with his brother George in the World Beater, went on to new fortunes at the Bullfrog-Rhyolite strikes and later at Skidoo. The Ballarat post office closed in 1917, making official the death of the town that had really succumbed two years before. The Clair family bought the Ratcliff, and the site of the mine is now known as Clair Camp. The tailings of the Ratcliff were worked by W. D. Clair starting in 1930; his efforts were quite successful, bringing out about $60,000 more in

Adobe ruins at Ballarat; western slopes of the Panamint Range form the backdrop.

gold. Total production for the mines in the Ballarat area totaled almost $1 million.

One of Ballarat's key citizens was Chris Wicht, who arrived in town in 1899 and owned the most popular saloon. It featured a pool table that had been brought around Cape Horn to San Francisco, from there to Panamint, and finally to Ballarat. Wicht died at age eighty in 1944, having drunk himself to death, according to writer George Pipkin.

Shorty Harris (see Shorty Harris and Harrisburg entries, Chapter 2) lived his last years as the sole resident of the ghost town of Ballarat until his death in 1934. The cemetery north of town features the grave of another well-known Death Valley character, Charles Ferge, better known as "Seldom Seen Slim," who claimed he hadn't taken a bath in twenty years because water was too scarce to "waste." On his tombstone is his response to the most common question a Death Valley prospector is ever asked: "Me lonely? Hell, no! I'm half coyote and half wild burro!"

Ballarat, long forgotten as a place for news, had one more moment in the spotlight in 1969. At Barker Ranch in Goler Wash, 22 miles away, Charles Manson and his "family" were captured. This was the nearest town to the ranch, so, for a second time in its history, the doings at the remote desert community of Ballarat received national attention.

Grave of "Seldom Seen Slim" at the Ballarat cemetery

Capsule Summary

MAJOR SITES

Keane Wonder Mine—spectacular walk with tramway, mining remnants

Chloride City—excellent one-stamp mill; walls, foundations, and debris

Death Valley Ranch—interesting mansion and grounds

TOPOGRAPHIC MAP INFORMATION FOR CHAPTER TWO:
SPIRITS OF DEATH VALLEY
(For map-reading assistance, consult Appendix A.)

Town	Topo Map Name	Size	Year	Importance*
Death Valley Ranch	Ubehebe Crater [a]	15'	1957	3
Stovepipe Well	Stovepipe Wells NE	7½'	1988 prv [b]	3
Harmony Borax Works	Furnace Creek [c]	15'	1952	3
Graves of Dayton and Harris	Badwater	7½'	1986 prv [b]	3
Eagle Borax Works	Badwater	7½'	1986 prv [b]	3
Ashford Mill	Shore Line Butte	7½'	1984	3
Leadfield	Grapevine Peak [d]	15'	1957	2
Chloride City	Chloride City	7½'	1988 prv [b]	2
Keane Wonder Mine	Chloride City	7½'	1988 prv [b]	2
Ryan	Ryan	7½'	1988 prv [b]	3
Death Valley Junction	Death Valley Junction	7½'	1987 prv [b]	3
Skidoo	Emigrant Canyon	7½'	1986 prv [b]	2
Harrisburg	Wildrose Peak	7½'	1988 prv [b]	3
Wildrose Kilns	Telescope Peak	7½'	1988 prv [b]	3
Panamint	Panamint	7½'	1988 prv [b]	2
Ballarat	Ballarat	7½'	1988 prv [b]	2

[a]—will be replaced by Scottys Castle 7½'
[b]—provisional edition (see Appendix A, "Distinguishing Characteristics")
[c]—will be replaced by Furnace Creek 7½'
[d]—will be replaced by Thimble Peak 7½'

*1—essential to find and/or enjoy site to fullest
 2—helpful but not essential
 3—unnecessary to find and enjoy site

SECONDARY SITES

Panamint—mill stack, foundations, and walls

Skidoo—superb mill; only debris at townsite

Ballarat—parched desert town with adobe remnants

Leadfield—tin buildings in dramatic setting

Wildrose Charcoal Kilns—well-constructed, well-preserved kilns

Harrisburg—Pete Aguereberry's home and outbuildings

Death Valley Junction—cemetery, deserted buildings, and the Amargosa Opera House

Harmony Borax Works—displays and remnants; visit Furnace Creek Ranch as well

Ryan—no trespassing; bring binoculars

MINOR SITES

Ashford Mill—walls, foundations

Eagle Borax Works—one ruin

Graves of Jimmy Dayton and Shorty Harris—touching grave site

Old Stovepipe Well—historic marker

ROAD CONDITIONS

Old Stovepipe Well, Keane Wonder Mine, Skidoo—dirt roads suitable for passenger cars

Chloride City, Eagle Borax Works, graves of Jimmy Dayton and Shorty Harris—unpaved roads; truck recommended

Leadfield—sandy road; truck or four-wheel drive vehicle recommended

Panamint—four-wheel drive vehicle recommended

All other sites—paved roads

TRIP SUGGESTIONS

You will need several days to explore Death Valley ghost towns and historic sites. Round-trip mileage will be given from either Stovepipe Wells Village or Furnace Creek Ranch, which are about 25 miles apart and which have the most extensive facilities for lodging and camping. The first two trips are for those who wish to stay primarily on paved roads or very tame dirt roads. The next six trips can be added to the first two and are principally for trucks and/or four-wheel drive vehicles.

TRIP 1: Death Valley Ranch, Old Stovepipe Well, Harmony Borax Works and Furnace Creek Ranch, Ryan. This route will show you the best easy-to-reach sites in Death Valley. Round trip from Stovepipe Wells Village, about 160 miles.

TRIP 2: Harrisburg/Aguereberry Camp, Wildrose Charcoal Kilns, Ballarat. These are the most accessible sites on the western fringe of Death Valley. Round trip from Stovepipe Wells Village, 135 miles.

TRIP 3: Add Skidoo to Trip 2. A passenger car can take this eight-mile journey up to the townsite. Only a truck should explore from there.

TRIP 4: Add Panamint to Trip 2. Add about 22 miles (and two to three hours) in your four-wheel drive vehicle.

TRIP 5: Leadfield (California) and Rhyolite and Bullfrog (Nevada). Recommended only for truck or four-wheel drive vehicles, this spectacular excursion will cover about 105 miles round trip from Furnace Creek Ranch and will require about half a day if you take your time. (Note: A trip to Rhyolite and Bullfrog alone would be on paved roads.)

TRIP 6: Add Chloride City to Trip 5. You can take a side trip to Chloride City on your way to Lead-field. This truck/passenger car road (see directions, Chloride City entry) will add about 25 miles. Plan on spending a couple of hours.

TRIP 7: Add Keane Wonder Mine to Trips 1, 5, or 6. Add two-and-a-half to three hours to your day if you take the magnificent hike to the mine itself. Additional car mileage is only 5.4 miles to Trips 5 or 6 and about 17 miles to Trip 1.

TRIP 8: Graves of Jimmy Dayton and Shorty Harris, Eagle Borax Works, Ashford Mill. This 90-mile round trip from Furnace Creek Ranch includes the West Side Road, which consists of 40 miles of dirt and sand definitely for trucks only.

TRIP 9: Combine trips in this chapter with ones in: Chapter One—Keeler is less than 70 miles from Stovepipe Wells Village; and Chapter Three—Ballarat is about 60 miles northeast of the Randsburg-area ghost towns, and Furnace Creek Ranch is approximately 115 miles from Baker, which is a point on the loop of Trip 1 in Chapter Three.

TRIP 10: Death Valley Junction. Death Valley Junction is 27 miles north of Shoshone and 29 miles southeast of Furnace Creek Ranch. It is most logically visited on a trip along the eastern fringe of Death Valley or to or from Baker, a point on the loop of Trip 1 in Chapter Three.

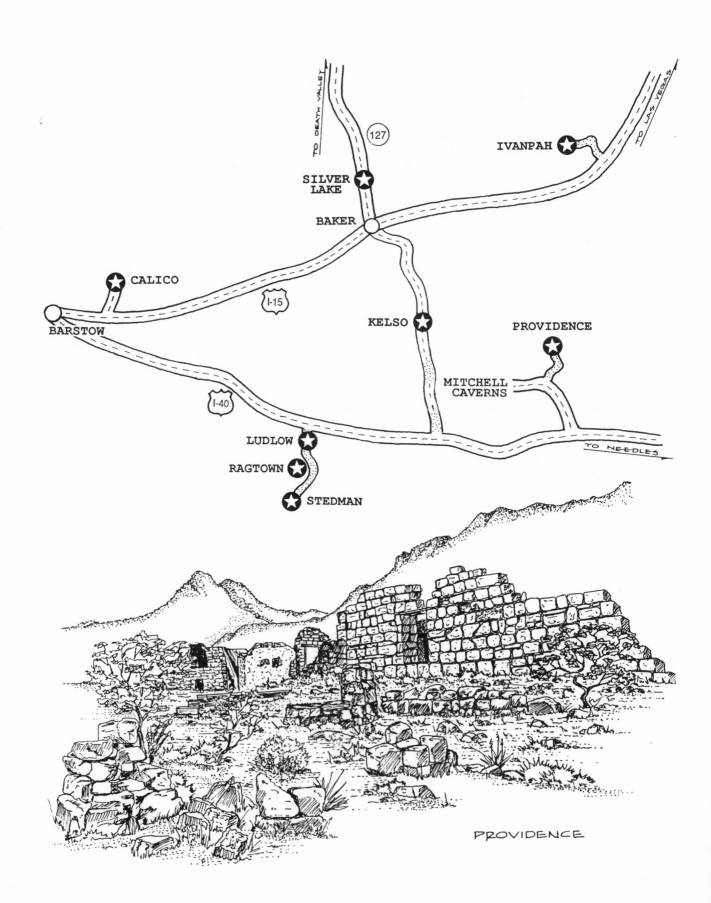

TO DEATH VALLEY

TO LAS VEGAS

(127)

IVANPAH

SILVER
LAKE

BAKER

CALICO

I-15

KELSO

PROVIDENCE

BARSTOW

MITCHELL
CAVERNS

I-40

LUDLOW

RAGTOWN

TO NEEDLES

STEDMAN

PROVIDENCE

3. Ghosts of the Mojave and the Kern

The Kern River and the Mojave Desert are the dominant topographic features that affected the ghost towns in this region. Named in 1845 by explorer John C. Fremont in honor of his topographer Edward M. Kern (who almost drowned in its waters), the Kern River was the site of a mad gold scramble in 1855 as hopeful prospectors cried, "Ho! for Kern River!"

The Mojave Desert has presented two challenges—to mine it and to cross it. As important as the desert mineral strikes were at places like Providence and Calico, even more memorable in California history were the treks across the Mojave Desert by mule teams heading to such famous bonanzas as Cerro Gordo, Bodie, and Death Valley.

For historical detail beyond what this chapter includes, consult *Ghost Towns of the Upper Mojave Desert,* by Alan Hensher and Larry Vredenburgh; *Early Days in Kern,* by Eugene Burmeister; *A California Middle Border,* by William Harland Boyd; and *Once Upon a Desert,* edited by Patricia Jernigan Keeling, as well as other books mentioned in this chapter.

Area One: East and Northeast of Barstow

CALICO

Calico is 11.4 miles northeast of Barstow. Drive east on I-15 and head north on Ghost Town Road.

If you're looking for a genuine ghost town, you know you're in a bit of trouble when you see "CALICO" in large letters on the side of a mountain, reminiscent of the old sign in the foothills above Hollywood. Calico is not the genuine article. But it is an entertaining spot to visit as long as you're willing to accept a place long on yarns and short on authenticity.

In 1881 Hulse Thomas, Tom Warden, George Yager, and G. Frank Mecham were leaving Grapevine Station (near Waterman, which preceded Barstow) and heading for a peak to the northeast. When John Peterson found out where they were going, he

referred to the peak as "calico-colored"; the peak, the range, and the subsequent town had a name.

The four prospectors discovered the deposits that became the Silver King Mine, the biggest silver producer in California in the 1880s. It and about sixty other mines yielded a total of between $13 and $20 million, making Calico the greatest of the Southern California silver towns. During fifteen years of prosperity, more than $86 million in silver was taken from the mines surrounding Calico. Between 1883 and 1885, San Bernardino County yielded almost $6 million in silver, which was about eighty-five percent of the total for the entire state; the Calico Mining District made up the bulk of the county's total. During the peak year of production, 1890, various mills totaling 150 stamps were producing ore worth about $200,000 per month. The boom was over in 1896. The major ore body played out, and the Silver Purchase Act devalued silver from a price of $1.13 per troy ounce in 1894 to a mere $.57 two years later.

Silver was not the only commodity mined in the area, however; a few years after the original silver discovery, colemanite borate deposits were found near Calico. These borate mines proved to be more valuable than the ones in Death Valley because of the ease of transporting the borate, as the mines were only 12 miles from the railroad at Daggett.

The San Bernardino City and County Directory of 1886 reported that Calico's current population was 1,200, with approximately fifty students in the school and regular church services every sabbath. The town had a deputy sheriff, two constables, a minister, two doctors, two lawyers, a justice of the peace, and five commissioners. In addition to the school, the town featured a post office; a Wells Fargo and Company express office; telephone and telegraph service; and a newspaper, described by the city and county directory as "ingeniously christened the Calico *Print,*" which "has a good circulation and is much prized as an exchange for the full and reliable news which it contains in its mining reviews." The paper also served Providence, Ivanpah, Mescal, Alvord, Orogrande, Death Valley, Daggett, and Barstow.

The San Bernardino City and County Directory, not surprisingly, conveniently overlooked some elements of the community. In addition to the refinements mentioned above, the town also featured a red-light district and the usual saloons and gambling parlors. Nevertheless, Calico was, overall, a

Wall Street in Calico on one of its more ghostlike days—nearly abandoned on Christmas Eve

rather orderly place that seemed to avoid the violence common to Western mining camps. Gambling, cock fighting, and drinking, although present, were not prevalent; the town seemed to place an emphasis on hard work, honesty, and the traditional values of the family.

By the peak year of 1890, Calico had a population estimated as high as 3,500. Along Wall Street—the main thoroughfare—pink adobe buildings housed boardinghouses, restaurants, stores, assay offices, and a shoe-and-boot shop that featured its own bar. One of the town's most popular residents was Dorsey, a black-and-white German shepherd that faithfully delivered the mail to the nearby Bismarck mines. The population of Calico was truly international, with citizens of American, Chinese, English, Cornish, Irish, Greek, French, and Dutch backgrounds.

But the crash in silver prices changed everything for prosperous Calico. Only ten years after the San

Bernardino's directory boasted of its many refinements, Calico was a ghost. Many of the buildings were moved to Barstow, Daggett, and Yermo. For an excellent historical photo of Calico before its luck ran out, see Donald Miller's *Ghost Towns of California,* page 27. The same nearly deserted street in the 1930s is shown in Paher's *Death Valley Ghost Towns,* page 43. The closest I could come is the nearly deserted Calico (shown above) on what must be one of its lowest attendance days of the year—Christmas Eve.

A cyanide plant was built in about 1915 to attempt to recover silver from the Silver King dumps. Walter and Cordelia Knott were homesteading at nearby Newberry at that time. Mr. Knott was one of the workers who constructed the redwood cyanide tanks and later kept an eye on Calico after it became a ghost town, sadly watching its deterioration. In 1951 the Knotts, now well known for their orchards, jellies, and Knott's Berry Farm, pur-

Original commercial building, now called Lane's General Store, in Calico.

Now known as Lucy Lane's house, this was once Calico's post office and courtroom.

chased the property and began to restore it; they subsequently donated the town to San Bernardino County in 1966. There is no fee to enter present-day Calico, but there are several tourist attractions that charge admission.

Over-restoration is Calico's shortcoming. The elaborate gingerbread and false-front buildings that now line Wall Street are closer to what tourists expect of the Old West than anything that was ever really there. But among the showy structures are a few unprepossessing ones that are all but overlooked; ironically, *they* are the originals. Some

Original adobe building of old Calico

have been renovated, some altered, and some left in decay. Seek these out for a look at old Calico: Lil's Saloon; the town office, surrounded by a picket fence; Lucy Lane's house, which originally was the post office and courtroom; Smitty's Gallery; the general store; and the ruin identified as Joe's Saloon. One of my favorite buildings is a faithful reconstruction—the schoolhouse.

At the south end of the parking lot on the west is the road to the cemetery. You will find some excellent weathered gravemarkers such as the one that reads:

Stone ruin at Calico; street lamp, hitching post, and signs are modern embellishments.

RIP

BABY FELIX SWAN

DIED JULY 5, 1895

FOUR DAYS OLD

Incidentally, the miners who discovered silver in the 1880s were not, by any means, the earliest visitors to the area. Six miles due east of the Calico townsite is an archaeological site, open to the public, that has been in the process of excavation since 1965. Since then more than 11,400 stone tools have been found. It is possible that prehistoric man may have used the site as a quarry, a workshop, or even a campsite as far back as 200,000 years ago.

LUDLOW, RAGTOWN, AND STEDMAN

Ludlow is 50 miles east of Barstow off I-40. Ragtown in 4.9 miles south of Ludlow on the main dirt road. Stedman is 2.8 miles south of Ragtown.

Ludlow was a railroad town, originally a water stop for the Atlantic and Pacific Railroad that came across the desert in 1882. Later, the townsite took on additional importance as a supply stop with the discov-

Calico cemetery

Completed in 1955, this replica of the Calico schoolhouse stands on the location of the original.

Wooden marker at the Calico cemetery

ery of ore in the hills to the south in the late 1880s. The town was named for William B. Ludlow, who was a master car-repairer for the Atlantic and Pacific Railroad. From the town branched two additional short lines—the Tonopah and Tidewater, and the Ludlow and Southern. Both lines connected with the Atchison, Topeka and Santa Fe Railroad, which had taken over the route in 1897.

The Tonopah and Tidewater Railroad was the child of Francis Marion "Borax" Smith and the Pacific Coast Borax Company in Death Valley. The name of the "T & T" signified its projected limits—from Tonopah, Nevada, to the tidewater of the Pacific Ocean at San Diego. In reality it was on a considerably smaller scale; when completed in 1907, it ran only from Ludlow to Beatty, Nevada, a distance of 169 miles. When the line was combined with the Bullfrog Goldfield Railroad in 1908, the route added 78 more miles.

Celestia Gilliam, who grew up in the area, reported in *Once Upon a Desert* that the T & T had no hoboes riding it because "it didn't go anyplace." She also said that the railroad's handcarts were frequently used on unofficial occasions, such as for shopping trips, joyrides, and "courting purposes."

The second branch railroad at Ludlow, owned by the Ludlow and Southern Railway Company, had a ten-mile run that took about forty minutes to head south to the Bagdad Chase Mines at Stedman. In about 1898 John Suter, a Santa Fe roadmaster, found copper and gold deposits in the Bullion Mountains while looking for water. He and about a dozen employees were working his claim, the Bagdad, up until about 1900; a year later he sold his operation to four New Yorkers, and the site became a part of a conglomeration of claims known as the Bagdad Chase Mine.

The town at the site was originally called Rochester, or Camp Rochester, for the New York hometown of two of the major backers, J. H. Stedman and Benjamin Chase. Obviously, Chase supplied part of the name for the mine while Stedman contributed the eventual name for the town. The site was also known informally as "Copenhagen" because of all the Danes and Swedes working the mine. E. H. Stagg was the general manager of the mining operation, which probably accounts for the fact that the original post office, granted to Camp Rochester in 1902, was called Stagg. The railroad was completed in June 1903, at a cost of $80,000, to take

ore from Camp Rochester to the A, T & S F main line at Ludlow and from there to Barstow for milling.

A photograph of Camp Rochester in David Myrick's *Railroads of Nevada,* volume two (pp. 832–33), shows the Bagdad Chase Gold Mining Company Store; an engine house; several mine structures, including at least five headframes; and over two dozen wood buildings that likely were residences. Despite its small size, Myrick reports that from 1880 to 1970 the mine produced one half of all the gold mined in San Bernardino County. But Camp Rochester was not a lively spot. E. H. Stagg ran a tight town, and no liquor was allowed. Ludlow, then, became the "blow-off" town for the thirsty, recreation-starved miners.

What did Ludlow have to offer them? Much of the town was owned by the Murphy Brothers, who at one point had a restaurant, store, warehouse, and garage. More of Ludlow was the property of Mother Preston, who owned at least eight buildings along Main Street, immediately north of the railroad tracks: a store, hotel, boarding house, saloon, cafe, no fewer than three dwellings, and a pool hall. Mother Preston was a good businesswoman and reportedly a talented poker player. After she sold out her properties to the Murphy Brothers, she retired to France. A very helpful map, reproduced in Myrick's book (pp. 560–61), gives the whole layout of Ludlow, showing the routes of the three railroad lines as well as the locations of a dance hall, school, tennis courts, U.S. Route 66, gas stations, and various other commercial and residential buildings.

From Myrick's book also comes my favorite Ludlow anecdote: Goldfield, Nevada, considered itself a sophisticated city with subtle tastes, so an entrepreneur there ordered a shipment of frogs' legs from the Gulf Coast sent via railway express. The delicacy arrived in Ludlow on the Santa Fe to make connection via the Tonopah and Tidewater railroad to Goldfield. Alas, the connection was missed, and the frogs' legs were in danger of spoiling. To cut losses, the legs were sold three for a dollar in Ludlow. The dish proved so popular among the townspeople that subsequent shipments also "missed connections" until a suspicious railway express investigator discovered what was going on and put a stop to it. For a short time, though, Ludlow's culinary fare rivaled San Francisco's.

Ludlow prospered largely because of the junction of the three railroads, and the Tonopah and Tidewater was especially important as the railroad's offices and shops were located there. The closing of operations of the Pacific Coast Borax Company in Death Valley in 1927–28 initiated the decline of the T & T, and the Depression guaranteed its death. The line ceased operation between Ludlow and Crucero, 25 miles north, in 1933, and in that year the rail-yard shops were moved to Death Valley Junction. Even that shortened line shut down in 1940; the rails were torn up, beginning in Beatty in July 1942 and finishing in Ludlow twelve months later.

The Ludlow and Southern Railroad had been long gone by then. It had ceased commercial operations in 1916, and the tracks had been maintained solely for the use of an occasional "speeder." The rails were torn up in 1935 and were reputed to have been sent to the Philippines for use on a sugar plantation.

The loss of the two branch lines, of course, also spelled decline for Ludlow. The town that at one time consisted of two commercial blocks and a population of about 500 began to die. Now Ludlow is a ghost town of two eras. Remains of the first, along the railroad tracks that are still the Santa Fe's, include the shell of the two-story Ludlow Mercantile Company (originally Mother Preston's, later the property of the Murphy Brothers) and a nearby abandoned wooden building.

On the south side of the tracks is a sadly deteriorating cemetery. The second and more modern ghost town has been caused by the presence of I-40. Ludlow, in addition to being a railroad town, was a

Wood frame buildings north of the tracks at Ludlow

The Ludlow Cafe, a ghost from a second era: it was a casualty as U.S. Route 66 was superceded by I-40, bypassing Ludlow.

stop along U.S. Route 66, and straddling the old, now bypassed highway are several closed businesses, including a recent casualty, the Ludlow Cafe, which still has booths, tables, and a lunch counter.

Heading on a dirt road south, along the old Ludlow and Southern railroad grade, you will come to the site of Ragtown, marked by an E Clampus Vitus plaque. Ragtown, with some faint remnants of the Old Pete Mine on Swede Hill, was a smaller sister to Stedman (aka Camp Rochester), which is almost three miles farther down the road. At Stedman you will find evidence of recent mining as well as tailings and dumps of older diggings.

Rumor continues to fuel hopes in the Stedman District. Although only two dilapidated buildings stand among the considerable diggings at the Bagdad Chase Mine, Ludlow has abounded with stories of the mine's reopening to work for gold "very soon."

1908 Ludlow Mercantile—note sign on wall: "Groceries, Meat Market, Liquors."

KELSO

Kelso is 22 miles north of the Amboy-Kelso exit on I-40, which is about 30 miles east of Ludlow. It is also 37 miles southeast of the Baker exit on I-15. The road to Kelso is listed on the topographic map as Kelbaker Road.

Kelso is one of the more pleasant surprises on the backroads of Southern California. Even when I visited it a second time, it still took me a moment to believe what I was seeing. No matter which direction you come from, you cross some of the Mojave Desert's most wide open spaces—and there it is, an outpost in the sand, with its two-story train depot dominating the tiny town the way a cathedral does in a small hamlet in Europe.

Union Pacific's boarded-up Kelso Depot

Kelso came to life because of the railroad and could have died from it as well. It was named for a railroad official when a siding was placed at the site in 1906, the year the San Pedro, Los Angeles, and Salt Lake Railroad (later taken over by the Union Pacific) extended a line to connect those cities. Gold and silver deposits were later discovered east of the townsite, on the west slope of the Providence Range. That area, which was named the Kelso District, included such mines as the Frisco Group, the Equitibus Group, and the Globe Mine.

The magnificent and graceful mission-style depot was built in 1925. During World War II, more than 2,000 people lived in Kelso and the surrounding area, where iron-ore mines such as Kaiser Steel's

Vulcan Mine were aiding the war effort. The station was truly the center of the community, as it was also used for trials, church services, and even dances and Christmas parties.

Although Kelso is still on the main line and plenty of rail traffic roars through, there is no reason to stop. The Vulcan Mine shut down in July 1946 because of an increasing sulfur content in the ore body and rising costs. Moreover, the steam engines that used to take on water for the dry, hot route ahead were replaced by diesel engines. As a result, the Union Pacific decided in the mid-1980s to raze the depot. A group of concerned citizens, led by Elden Hughes of East Los Angeles, moved to save the station. They formed the nonprofit Kelso Depot Fund to raise money for the upkeep of the building, since the Union Pacific graciously agreed to donate it to the group once that maintenance money is assured. The organization hopes for $250,000 to restore the building so that it can serve as a railroad museum, restaurant, and conference center.

In addition to the spectacular depot, with its long brick platform and its elms and palms shading a cool oasis from the desert sun, there are a post office and store (closed but for rent at this writing), a school (now a private residence), and a couple of old homes. On the south side of the tracks stand some mobile homes, inhabited principally by railroad employees.

Former Kelso post office

Assay office of the Bonanza King Mine, looking down at the road into Providence and the Colton Hills

The western states are filled with trackside foundations where depots used to be, and railfans and history buffs can only look at old photographs and mourn the passing of the actual buildings. But here at Kelso one station can be saved. This is a most worthy effort.

PROVIDENCE

To reach Providence, leave Interstate 40 at the Mitchell Caverns and Essex exit. Drive 10.4 miles north, going past the road to Hole in the Wall Recreation Area. Just .4 miles after you pass under a large utility line there is a road to the right with a sign for the Blair Ranch. Drive 5 miles up that dirt road. Immediately after crossing a wide, normally dry wash you will come to a fork in the road. The right, marked "private road," proceeds to the Blair Ranch; the left heads to Providence. The townsite remnants are 1.9 miles from this junction.

You will be heading west; the road that proceeds west-northwest goes to the Silver King Mine, where there are three standing buildings.

Pioneers traveling west most likely named the Providence Mountains because of the numerous springs that refreshed them through this often hot, arid country. The springs were an answer to a prayer—an act of Providence. Later, when silver deposits were found in those mountains in the spring of 1880, the name was also given to the town that developed next to the biggest discovery, the Bonanza King Mine. During one eighteen-month period, the Bonanza King was reported to have yielded almost $1 million in silver. By 1883 Providence was a full-fledged town including a post office, two general stores, a saloon, and two hotels. Production dropped as silver prices slipped, and the mine closed in

March of 1885. The Bonanza King reopened a couple of times, but the peak days were over. The post office closed in 1892. Two revivals of the mine occurred in 1906–07 and 1915–20.

Providence—walls of the block stone assay office of the Bonanza King Mine

Nearly a dozen rock foundations now hide in the desert scrub, along with several easily visible rock walls. The largest is a building made of white rock blocks cut from a nearby ledge, which was the assay office for the Bonanza King Mine, according to Mitchell Caverns Ranger Barry Menges. On my two visits I saw evidence of recent claim work— marked bags and core samples—just west of the assay office. If the work remains, do not disturb it. When I was there the road to the mine was clearly posted against trespassing, so I looked at that portion of the site from behind the sign.

I love Providence. The mountains provide a wonderful backdrop, and the valley air is so clear that I could see fog along the Colorado River, some 45 miles away. On my first visit, in winter, nights were crisp and clean, but cold and often windy. During the summer the days can be formidable. But when I was there on a second visit in early May, the temperature was perfect and the solitude was complete.

SILVER LAKE

The remains of Silver Lake are 8 miles north of Baker on state route 127.

Only a cemetery—with the grave of Harry Nickerson, "Death Valley Jack"—and one standing adobe

ruin framed by dusty trees can attest to the existence of Silver Lake, a town that had saloons, a post office, a depot with a telegraph office, boarding houses, and a population of about a hundred in 1907. The dances that "Ma" Palmer put on in her tent-roofed establishment were principal attractions back then.

The town existed because it was on the line of the Tonopah and Tidewater Railroad, which extended its tracks across the dry Silver Lake in March 1906. Later flooding proved that the lake wasn't always dry, and the tracks became submerged. At one time Silver Lake was the most important community in the area; if you lived in Baker and wanted a ticket on the Tonopah & Tidewater, you needed to travel to Silver Lake to buy it. Furthermore, all drinking water for Baker came from Silver Lake on the T & T. The town served as a supply point for the Riggs silver mines to the east and the Avawatz Mountains mines to the west and was on the main highway from Daggett to Las Vegas and from Ludlow to Shoshone.

The town began a rapid decline in the mid-1920s when the Arrowhead Trail Highway (U.S. 91, connecting Los Angeles to Salt Lake City) bypassed it. The post office was transferred to Baker in 1933, and the Tonopah and Tidewater ceased service in 1940.

As meager as the remains of Silver Lake are, they are considerable compared to those of the other Tonopah and Tidewater stops in the area. At Riggs, Valjean, and Sperry, all north of Silver Lake, nothing is left to indicate that they were ever there.

IVANPAH

Ivanpah is 6.6 miles west of the Yates Well exit on I-15. See the text for specific, detailed directions. Do not confuse this site with the railroad town of the same name southwest of Nipton.

Ivanpah was the first town located in the Mojave Desert and was the only real outpost of civilization in that area for thirty years. It was founded in 1870, a year after the Paiute Company of California and Nevada found silver deposits in the Clark (originally "Clarke") Mountains. The name Ivanpah came from a Southern Paiute word meaning "good (or clear, white) water," according to Gudde's *California Place Names*. The townsite, platted on 160 acres, was several miles down the canyon from the Paiute Company mines along a wash near an abun-

The lone adobe ruin that marks the site of Silver Lake

dant spring (the "good, clear water" that carried the original place-name—Ivanpah Spring).

Fifteen buildings, among them a hotel, two stores, adobe houses, and the Paiute Company headquarters, stood in Ivanpah by 1871. The mines were on Alaska Hill, over eight miles northwest of the townsite. The population of Ivanpah was 300 in the fall of 1872, but by 1875 it had dwindled to only 100 whites and 40 to 50 Indians as strikes in Darwin and Panamint (see entries, Chapters 1 and 2) had drawn men out of the Clark District.

The building of the Bidwell ten-stamp mill in 1876 signaled a resurgence of life in Ivanpah that lasted into 1879. In April of that year, the town featured two hotels, two blacksmith shops, two cobblers' shops, two hay yards, several houses, and a post office, which had opened in June 1878. The shipments of bullion from Ivanpah and the rest of the Clark District—bars weighing almost two hundred pounds of nearly pure silver—were bringing prosperity and progress to San Bernardino and Colton.

But by 1880 the glory days were over. Financial troubles of the mining companies, along with strikes in Providence (see entry, Chapter 3), helped empty the town. The voting rolls dropped from seventy-eight in 1879 to eight in 1886. The town was virtually deserted in 1892 except for Bidwell's store and boardinghouse; that store closed in 1898 and the post office followed a year later.

Two other sites have shared Ivanpah's name. The second Ivanpah was a railroad stop, about 12 miles from the original mining town, along the California Eastern Railway in 1902. When a railroad line (now the Union Pacific) was constructed in 1906 to connect Los Angeles and Salt Lake City, a town was built at the junction of that line and the California Eastern. It was called Leastalk, later South Ivanpah, and finally Ivanpah, the name of the present site southwest of Nipton.

Little remains at the original Ivanpah: one rock dugout, a wall of another building that one source

Stone dugout near Bidwell Mill site at Ivanpah

Rock wall at Ivanpah; Ivanpah Valley in the right background

says was a smelter, and a couple of nearby dumps stand at the Bidwell mill site. Between the two buildings is a shaft covered by wood, so use caution. Some traces of mining efforts can be seen in the surrounding hills.

To reach these remnants of Ivanpah, exit from I-15 at Yates Well, about 45 miles northeast of Baker near the California-Nevada border. Go west from the overpass, where you will come almost immediately to a "T" in the road. Note your mileage here. Turn right (north) along the road that was the old highway, now only partially paved. Follow the road where it veers to the left off the pavement (the pavement just heads to a fence). You will pass under a power line, but ignore the power-line road. When you come to a fork in the road 4.6 miles from the original "T" near the interstate, take the right and keep to the main dirt road. You will pass near a water tank and a small ruin. Beyond that ruin .3 miles, or 2 miles from the fork in the road and 6.6 miles from the "T," you will see on your left a cottonwood tree and, partially hidden by brush, an old corral made of railroad ties. If you have a truck, you can drive between the tree and the corral and proceed a short distance to the site of the Bidwell Mill, or you can leave your vehicle near the corral and walk in.

Ivanpah Spring can be seen .6 miles up the dirt road beyond the mill-area ruins of Ivanpah. There you will find walls and foundations near a cottonwood tree. You can also continue up the canyon on the main dirt road to see evidence of the mines themselves.

The best source for the story of Ivanpah is Hensher and Vredenburgh's compendium, *Ghost Towns of the Upper Mojave Desert* (see Bibliography). Most of the historical material in this entry was adapted from their work and is used with their permission.

Area Two: Randsburg and Environs

The ghost towns in the vicinity of Randsburg have an interconnected history; therefore, the entries in this section of Chapter Three are presented not in a logical geographic sequence, as is the case in the rest of this book, but rather in historical sequence. A particularly readable account of the history of this area can be found in Marcia Rittenhouse Wynn's *Desert Bonanza: The Story of Early Randsburg* (see Bibliography). Mrs. Wynn gives many per-

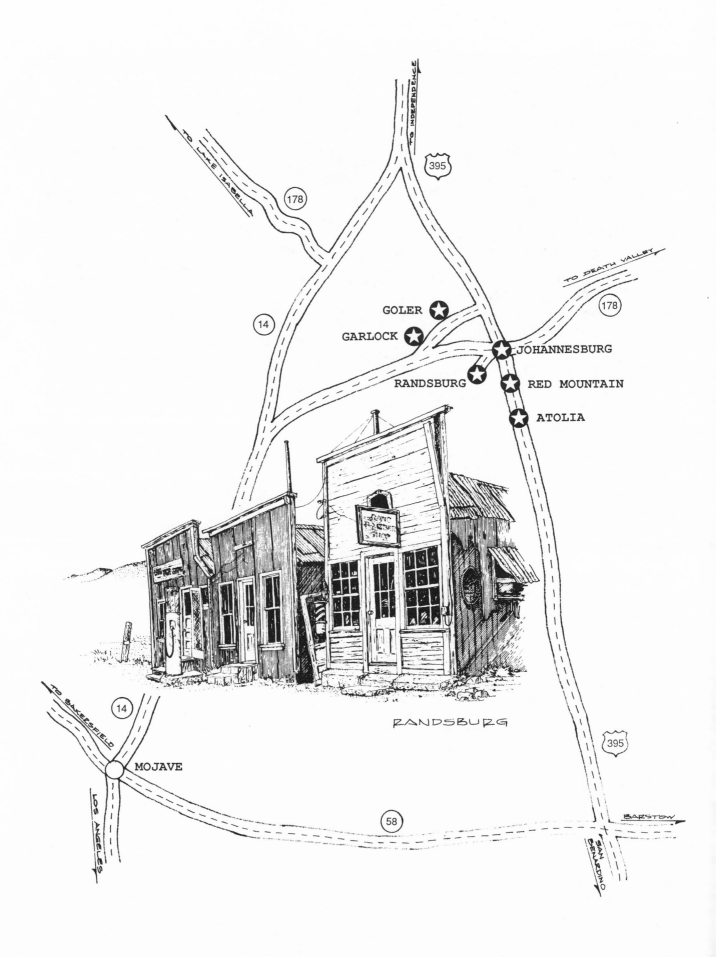

TO LAKE ISABELLA

TO INDEPENDENCE

395

178

TO DEATH VALLEY

14

178

GOLER ⭐

GARLOCK ⭐

JOHANNESBURG ⭐

RANDSBURG ⭐

RED MOUNTAIN ⭐

ATOLIA ⭐

RANDSBURG

TO BAKERSFIELD

14

MOJAVE

LOS ANGELES

58

BARSTOW

395

SAN BERNARDINO

sonal anecdotes, as she was born and raised in Randsburg. The book also features outstanding historical photographs.

GOLER

Goler is 5 miles northwest of Randsburg off the Goler Road, which intersects the Randsburg Road. The turnoff to Goler is 2.6 miles northeast of Garlock.

The discovery of gold in Goler Canyon in 1893 initiated prospecting in what was to become the Rand District, one of Southern California's richest finds. The name Goler was given to the site because some believed, almost certainly erroneously, that this was the location of the "lost" Goler (also, "Goller") Mine, which had been reported some forty-four years earlier. The Goler Mining District was formed in March 1893, with the first official claim called Jackass Placer.

These placer deposits caused the formation of a town and the opening of a stage route from Mojave. The most popular people in the small camp called Goler were Tom and Polly Duke, known as Uncle Tom and Aunt Polly, who ran a boardinghouse for the miners. The miners spread out in all directions, and it was from this vicinity that three of them ventured out and found the bonanza that was to become the Yellow Aster Mine, a discovery that transformed the area.

The best remnants at Goler today, visible from the highway, are ruins of a mill marked on the topographic map as the Yellow Aster. That, however, conflicts with other sources that state the Yellow Aster Mill was much nearer to Garlock. North of the mill ruins are some occupied buildings and a well that is identified on the same map as Benson Well.

RANDSBURG

Randsburg is about 63 miles northwest of Barstow just off U.S. 395 and about 37 miles northeast of Mojave.

Dr. Rose Burcham was trying to help get her husband cured of prospecting fever. A respected general practitioner in San Bernardino, she had grubstaked her husband, Charles Austin Burcham, former cattleman and meat-market owner, for two years of scratching in the desert, and his time was almost up. Along with companions John Singleton and Frederic M. Mooers, he was trying his luck several miles southeast of a small strike near Goler Wash.

The three prospectors hit promising ore and made claims on April 25, 1895. They protected their find, until the claims could be properly registered, with a very clever deception. They filled their wagon with worthless bull quartz and went into a nearby camp with their "find." Curious miners sneaked a look under the wagon's tarp. When their "ore" was examined, miners considered the trio to be fools and dismissed their claim. But their real samples certainly were not worthless. The claims originally were collectively called the Rand Mine, after Witwatersrand—commonly known as the Rand—a gold-producing district in South Africa. The settlement that formed around this fabulously rich claim became Rand Camp, later Randsburg; the mine's name was changed to the Yellow Aster, the title of a novel that Mooers had been reading.

Mining-camp histories are full of accounts of small-time miners who found a pocket only to see everyone else make the fortune, but the Yellow Aster is not a case in point, although it might have been. The three men were tempted to sell out early, but Dr. Rose Burcham did not trust any of the offers of outside money trying to buy into the claim. She wanted them to retain total control over the entire mining operation and remained firm despite many offers of capital. Rose Burcham was used to having to exert her influence in traditionally male fields; after all, she was a medical doctor when a female in the profession was a rarity. More than one man walked away from her refusal of offers to buy into the Yellow Aster by proclaiming that he would never again try to have dealings with "that woman." Because of her intransigent good sense, all of them became millionaires.

Initially Rose Burcham served as bookkeeper, secretary, and cook; the three men worked the mine. Because of tales of highwaymen, the first gold brick that came from the Yellow Aster was delivered in person to Mojave, 35 miles away, by Mooers, who drove a wagon, accompanied by Dr. Burcham, who carried the treasure in her lap.

The operation proved far too large for such a small work force. By 1899 the Yellow Aster was employing 150 men with a payroll exceeding $13,000 per month. According to Mrs. Wynn in *Desert Bonanza,* Dr. Burcham retained the dominant role in the running of the mine, and her influence permeated the operation: the hundred-stamp mill, for ex-

Randsburg—general store, adobe post office, and former union hall

ample, was spotless, and in the main engine room was a potted palm! Mrs. Wynn called Rose Burcham a "brilliant, business-like, crisp, hard working, exacting" person.

Naturally, as the Yellow Aster prospered and other claims were filed, the settlement nearby grew in kind. Randsburg was a mere camp in 1895; by the summer of 1896, the population was about 1,000. But by the winter of 1896–97 one account says there were some three hundred buildings and tents, not including "dugouts, stone houses, and shacks." By the turn of the century, more than 3,500 people lived in Randsburg, and the *Randsburg Miner* claimed in an article at the time that by the close of 1900, some $3,000,000 worth of gold had been taken from the district.

Randsburg was primarily a company town, so it was spirited but not rowdy. But it was also the scene of some fierce labor strife. Unions attempted to make the Yellow Aster a fully unionized mine, and one strike lasted from 1902 until 1916. Production continued with nonunion miners, however. At one

point relations were so strained that on Saturday nights two dances were held in town, union and nonunion, and girls who were seen at one party were not welcome at the other.

Randsburg contains several buildings worth examining, and it certainly is the best ghost town in the area. A good starting point when you arrive in Randsburg is the post office, which was made of adobe for protection against recurring fires. On the right of the post office is a corrugated false front, formerly the old union hall that was the headquarters for the labor movement. Across the street stands the White House Saloon, which has a huge bar built by thirsty Yellow Aster carpenters. A door in the basement of the White House opened into a tunnel that led toward the Yellow Aster; local opinion holds that it was used for high-grading the mine. Several small false fronts, a church, and the interesting Randsburg Desert Museum (complete with mining equipment and a five-stamp mill), make up the rest of the main business section. The Yellow Aster is south of town and is closed to the public.

Three false fronts on Randsburg's main street, Butte Avenue

GARLOCK

Garlock is 12.8 miles east of state route 14.

Garlock's attraction was its ready supply of water. From the 1860s to the 1890s the place was called Cow Wells, and was a dependable watering stop out of Death Valley for prospectors and travelers. In late 1895, Eugene Garlock brought his eight-stamp mill from Tehachapi to process the ore that was being found at the Yellow Aster Mine in nearby Randsburg (see preceding entry), which did not at that time have a water supply sufficient to run a mill. A post office under the name of Garlock was granted in April 1896 with Ida Kelly as postmistress (see Red Mountain entry for more on the Kellys). The settlement eventually featured a store, a school, saloons, and many residences. The most imposing building was the Doty Hotel, where one guest wryly observed that from its second story "one could look farther and see less than at any point in the surrounding country."

Garlock prospered only until 1898, when it was

dealt two crippling blows: a railroad spur was constructed from Kramer to Johannesburg, and a waterline was extended from Goler Wash to Randsburg. No one needed their stamp mill; no one needed their water. The effect was that Garlock's population plummeted from several hundred in 1899 to a single resident in 1903. The post office closed in 1904. The town that once had a doctor, a two-story hotel, a baseball team, and a saloon with the wonderful name of Jerome Cheney's Thirst Emporium was dead.

Garlock had two brief resurrections. In 1911 railroad crews laying track between Mojave and Keeler lived in the empty town, and in the early 1920s a mine opened and a salt company began working the deposits of nearby Koehn Lake. Both of those projects failed, and the post office, which had reopened in 1923, closed for good in 1926. The most lasting effort in Garlock was the school, which served the children of Saltdale and surrounding communities from the 1920s until 1951.

Although Garlock flourished for only a very

Deserted building at Garlock; depending upon the source, either a stage station-store-bar or a brothel-saloon

short time, it has several items worth inspecting. On the east side of the highway is a substantial rock building, which author Norman Weis says is the Miller Building—formerly a stage station, a general store, and a bar. Roberta Martin Starry, in her informative history of the area, *Exploring the Ghost Town Desert,* claims that the building was a saloon and brothel. Across the highway is an historical marker, and, on the other side of a fence, a few old buildings, including one made from railroad ties. The most significant item is a fairly complete arrastre, which Starry says was mechanized, not mule drawn. About a dozen buildings from later eras, some occupied and some deserted, stand on either side of the old highway at the old site.

Arrastre at Garlock

JOHANNESBURG

Johannesburg is 2.1 miles east of Randsburg.

Johannesburg, commonly called "Joburg," is Randsburg's sister community and, like its neighbor, was named for a South African mining district. Johannesburg was the supply center for Randsburg's mining boom, and a strong rivalry developed between them. Randsburg's citizens could sneer that Johannesburg wouldn't have existed without their mines—that it lived in Randsburg's shadow; Joannesburg's populace, however, could retort that their town helped keep Randsburg alive because of the railroad that had its terminus in Joburg.

In addition, Johannesburg was a planned community, much more orderly looking than the random layout of Randsburg. It was a family town with a water system extending to the residences. The Laurestina Club, a social organization whose refinements surpassed anything in Randsburg, had its own clubhouse featuring a billiard table, piano, and facilities for dances, card parties, and dinners for members. The town itself had the usual commercial enterprises, such as boardinghouses, lumberyards, a post office, lunch counters, two saloons, and a music hall. Citizens could rightfully boast that the largest building in the Randsburg area was, in fact, in Johannesburg—the two-story Johannesburg Hotel, which had between thirty-six and forty rooms, a bar, a billiard room, and a ladies' parlor.

A final refinement that Johannesburg could vaunt was its nine-hole golf course, which the *Randsburg Miner* reported in 1900 as beginning at the Red Dog Mill, running clear around town, crossing the railroad twice, and returning to the Red Dog. The *Miner* also remarked that the course had nine greens and thirteen members.

The Red Dog Mill was a dominant structure in Johannesburg. It could be seen up on the hill above town and heard from all over as its stamps crushed ore (five stamps from that mill stand on the property of the Desert Museum in Randsburg). Imagine a serene, relaxing game of golf commencing near the considerable din of a stamp mill.

The key ingredient of the town, originally, was the railroad. The 28.5-mile rail connection built by the Randsburg Railway Company from the A, T & S F main line in Kramer was begun in October of 1897 and completed by Christmas of the same year. Regular service began on January 5, 1898, with talk of extending the line all the way to Keeler or to

Johannesburg cemetery and the headframe of the King Solomon Mine

Death Valley—survey work was even done to Ballarat. But the main reason for the railroad was the Yellow Aster Mine in Randsburg, for the rail link enabled the huge mine to send its ore to Barstow to the fifty-stamp mill of the Randsburg-Santa Fe Reduction Company. That contract, however, expired in 1899, and in February of that year the Yellow Aster built its own 130-stamp mill; the Randsburg Railway Company had lost its principal customer. The line was sold to the Santa Fe in 1903; it was abandoned in 1933, and the tracks were torn up one year later.

The town today shows little evidence of the past. If there's still a golf course, it must be one enormous sand trap. Most original buildings that still exist have been renovated and are occupied. The street names echo some of the most famous mines of the West—Comstock, Panamint, Saint Elmo. The principal ghost town attraction is the cemetery, sitting at the southwest corner of the town, with the King Solomon Mine (discovered in 1896 and last active in 1942) providing a backdrop. Here you will find the grave of William Henry "Burro" Schmidt, who became famous in "Ripley's Believe It or Not" as the man who, with the help of his two burro companions Jack and Jenny, tunneled through 1,872

feet of mountain over a period of thirty-two years. The initial reason for the tunnel was to send ore through it from his mine for transportation to a smelter, but by the time he completed his digging in 1938, the tunnel was pretty much an end in itself. There wasn't ore to move, and Schmidt didn't seem to care much. He was sixty-eight; his remarkable project was finished, so he sold his claims and moved. He died in 1954.

ATOLIA

Atolia is 2.9 miles south of Red Mountian on U.S. 395.

Just as gold was playing out in Randsburg, rich deposits of tungsten were discovered in 1905 or 1907 on the southern fringe of the hill named, appropriately, Red Mountian. The tungsten, which is used in steel alloy, was initially found in placer deposits, but subsequent shafts yielded rich veins of scheelite, an ore of tungsten. At one time, the Atolia deposits made up the biggest producer of tungsten in the world. The Tungsten Mining Company gave the town its name, derived from two of its officers, Atkins and DeGolia. *California Place Names* states

Company residence at Atolia

that one source claims DeGolia supplied only the "-lia," and that the "o" in the name came from local miner Pete Osdick (see Red Mountain entry). The population rose to 2,000 as the town prospered between 1907 and 1915. Atolia featured such amenities as a dairy, a picture show, and the Bucket of Blood saloon, where scheelite was used for poker chips.

Not much remains to testify to Atolia's activity. "No trespassing" signs stand on both sides of the highway, but from your car you can still view the myriad shafts that dot the bleak landscape. A couple of buildings stand on the west side of the highway, and the mine on the east side shows definite signs of activity.

RED MOUNTAIN

Red Mountain is 1.5 miles south of Johannesburg on U.S. 395.

When the tungsten excitement abated in Atolia (see preceding entry), a new rush occurred to take its place. The annoying rock that gold miners had been trying to get past for years was assayed for its own worth in 1919 by two prospectors named Williams and Nosser. It was found to be almost pure horn silver. Various names are given for the big claims that resulted, and some of them are almost certainly for the same claim—California Rand Silver Mine, Rand Silver Mine, Big Silver Mine, Big Kelly Mine, and the Kelly Mine are all cited in various sources.

Mrs. Wynn, in *Desert Bonanza*, connects the name Kelly with the Rand Silver Mine. She says

that John and Ida Kelly, down on their luck after losing all their placer equipment due to flooding in Shasta County, were in Bakersfield, heading toward Mexico, when they heard about the diggings in Rand Camp (later Randsburg). They ended up in Garlock, where they served meals to teamsters traveling through town and to miners working their claims in the vicinity. Ida Kelly became Garlock's first postmistress, and her husband John became constable. They later moved to Randsburg, where he again served as constable; later he was sheriff of Kern County. Mrs. Wynn states that it was the Kellys, in 1919, who discovered the silver deposits at the Rand Silver Mine and made themselves a fortune.

No matter who was responsible for the strike, it certainly caused a rejuvenation of the Randsburg area. The news of rich silver deposits brought prospectors from all over. Empty buildings from Johannesburg, Randsburg, and even Garlock were moved to the new diggings. All that was needed was a name for the place. An unofficial one already existed: in 1905 the A, T & S F had named a station along their recently acquired Kramer-Johannesburg route for P. J. "Pete" Osdick, who with his brother had operated a stamp mill nearby. When a town began to form near the Rand—or Kelly—Silver Mine, Pete Osdick, who had been scratching for gold within a breath of all that silver, envisioned a town that would be quiet and orderly. And that town

School at Red Mountain

Red Mountain's Kelly Mine

would be named Osdick. You can imagine how well the idea of that sort of place was received by the miners who scrambled to the district. A second town was born immediately adjacent to Osdick that was the antithesis of temperance; it went by various names, including Inn City and Sin City.

The original post office for the two settlements was in the name of Osdick when it opened on Valentine's Day in 1922, but it was renamed Red Mountain in 1929 in a bureaucratic move that was aimed at putting an end to squabbling over names. The new name satisfied just about nobody; Pete Osdick, naturally, was distinctly dissatisfied—but the new name stuck. Osdick does live on, nevertheless, according to *California Place Names;* the name is still used for the school and voting districts.

But the spirit of Red Mountain was definitely from Sin City, not Osdick. It was advertised as a place ". . . where every night is Saturday night, and Saturday night is the Fourth of July." You could get a drink, they crowed, in any establishment except the post office. During Prohibition, the town was dry only when word of an impending raid came down the line. Bands came from Los Angeles to play, and the place lived on as a night spot long after the silver gave out.

The Kelly Mine produced more than $7 million in its first four years and was one of the richest silver deposits in Southern California. In fact, for several years it was the biggest producing silver mine in the United States. And today it is the Kelly headframe and mill that yield the richest results in Red Mountain for the ghost-town hunter. Also worth noting is the school, with its mission-tile-roofed bell tower. Several small company-town-type residences—most of them occupied—and some commercial structures comprise the remainder of the town.

Area Three: In and Around Antelope Valley

LLANO

Llano is 20 miles east of Palmdale on the Pearblossom Highway (state route 138) and 4.5 miles east of Pearblossom.

Mining towns, railroad towns—but a socialist-colony ghost town? As improbable as it may seem, such a place exists, abandoned for almost seventy

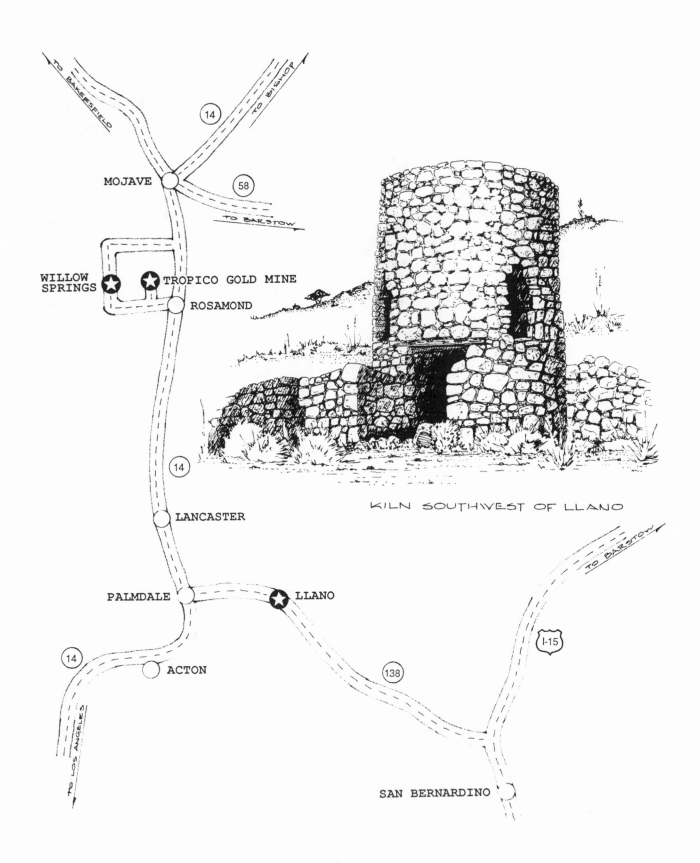

TO BAKERSFIELD

TO BISHOP

14

MOJAVE

58

TO BARSTOW

WILLOW SPRINGS

TROPICO GOLD MINE

ROSAMOND

14

LANCASTER

KILN SOUTHWEST OF LLANO

TO BARSTOW

PALMDALE

LLANO

I-15

14

ACTON

138

TO LOS ANGELES

SAN BERNARDINO

years, not far from Los Angeles and San Bernardino. I first learned about Llano (Spanish for "level field," "plain," or "even ground"), from a *Desert Magazine* dated May 1963. When I read the article, then almost twenty years old, I assumed that little, if anything, would remain of the site after the passage of that much time in an area that has experienced considerable growth. I was virtually assured of my belief when a friend of mine living in Palmdale told me that he had driven along the Pearblossom Highway countless times, and certainly no ghost town was there.

No ghost town, perhaps, in the Hollywood sense, but Llano most definitely is there. It has changed not at all from the descriptions and photographs in the *Desert Magazine* article, which explained that the Llano del Rio Cooperative Colony existed between 1914 and 1918.

Actually, this was the second community on the land. The first colonization of Llano had been made in about 1888, perhaps by Quakers. A post office was established in 1890 at the ranch house of L. G. Tilghman, and the formation of a school district soon followed. The principal concern of the area was water for crops, accounting for the organization of the Big Rock Creek Irrigation District.

The peak year for the first Llano was 1895, when about a hundred people lived in or near the community that featured the post office (now combined with a store), the school, and even a nearby doctor. But droughts and the failure of the irrigation projects dried up Llano, and the people began to desert the valley. The school at Llano dropped from thirty-three pupils in 1894 to only five in 1900 and then closed. The post office followed in 1900.

The ghost town you will be exploring is of the second colony, which was founded by Los Angeles lawyer and prominent socialist Job Harriman, who acquired the land and established the community to prove the socialist theory of cooperative living. Members purchased shares in the colony and were also paid at the rate of $4.00 per day; most transactions, however, were on paper, not in cash. The first building erected was a 150 foot × 50 foot hotel that housed bachelors as well as visitors to the colony. Also in the hotel were a barbershop, a printshop, a library, and an assembly-dining hall with two large fireplaces. The first crop planted was alfalfa, and the community eventually produced about ninety percent of what it was consuming, but not without effort. The fields being cultivated were loaded with

Chimneys and pillars of the hotel at Llano

stones, and on at least one occasion the hard times were reflected in the colonists' diet—carrots.

At its peak between 1915 and 1917, Llano had a population of 900, making it the largest town by far in Antelope Valley. A colony printing plant published a monthly magazine, the *Western Comrade,* and a weekly newspaper, the *Llano Colonist.* There was a dairy, and almost 2,000 acres of land were being cultivated. Other nonfarming enterprises included a steam laundry, a cannery, a cleaning-pressing-dyeing plant, a rug-making plant, and a soap-making factory. Education of the young was a priority, and social activities included swimming, music, riflery, team sports, and weekly dances.

But human nature caused problems at the colony. In the *Desert Magazine* article, former colony member Tony Vacik gave one reason why the colony failed to produce as it might have: "Some people just will not cooperate. Fourteen comrades would be assigned to a project and probably four of them would do all the work." A second problem was a shortage of water. Elaborate rock-lined ditches were to bring irrigation from Big Rock Creek, which fed from waters on the other side of the San Andreas fault. Unfortunately, the water flow wasn't anywhere near the amount required.

Harriman and other colony leaders, discouraged by the Antelope Valley prospects, bought 20,000 acres in western Louisiana in 1917 and named it Newllano. Soon most of the colonists left for the Louisiana colony. But the Louisiana experiment was not much more successful than the Antelope Valley one. Harriman eventually returned to California and died in 1925 at the age of sixty-four.

Exploring the Antelope Valley colony brings

Horse barn ruins at Llano

gratifying rewards. The best point of reference in Llano is the intersection of state route 138 and 165th Street. East of that intersection .5 miles, on the north side of the highway, are the four rock pillars and twin fifteen-foot chimneys that mark the site of the old hotel/dining room/meeting hall. Nearby are the remnants of the lined ditches that were to bring the irrigation water to the terraced fields adjacent to the hotel. Faint ridges of the terracing efforts can still be seen. North of the hotel are the long rock walls of the horse barn and two foundations of what appear to be storage areas with twelve compartments.

One-half mile south of the hotel, on the other side of the highway, are the largest ruins at Llano. The 300-ton-capacity concrete silo, some twenty-eight to thirty feet in height, is visible from the hotel ruins. You can reach it either by driving in from the highway or by going back to 165th Street and heading south for .5 miles. There a road pro-

Llano's dairy barn and concrete silo

ceeds east to the site. Along with the silo are the walls of the dairy barn, larger than the horse barn but similar in construction, with a concrete trough still running along the foot of one wall. The most complete building at the townsite, although also roofless, is just northwest of the dairy barn.

Llano lime kiln in Rancho de la Vista

Two other unusual features of Llano remain. Drive south from the highway along 165th Street. The foundations of the old school, only faintly visible, are on the right side of the road about .5 miles from the highway. But you are heading for better things. Continue on for 1.5 more miles; there the main road becomes Bob's Gap Road. You will continue south on the dirt road into Rancho de la Vista. Go south one mile and turn west on the dirt road. In .3 miles a stone lime kiln will come into view at the foot of a knoll about 200 yards off the road. Be sure to walk over for a closer look.

Now return to the intersection of the Rancho de la Vista road and Bob's Gap Road. This time turn right and proceed 2.1 miles toward Bob's Gap, a dramatic natural cut in Holcomb Ridge. On the east side of the road, tucked into the wall of the Gap, is a second, more elaborate lime kiln with a roofless building near its base. The kilns were used by the

Lime kiln at Bob's Gap near Llano

colony to produce the lime that was used in the mortar for the extensive ditches, walls, and foundations.

On your way back to highway 138, note the ultimate irony: the proposed utopia, Llano del Rio Cooperative Colony, died largely because of the hardships caused by the lack of water. Now millions of gallons of it pass across the southern border of the colony along the giant California Aqueduct.

TROPICO GOLD MINE

Drive west from Rosamond for 3 miles on Rosamond Blvd.; then turn north and follow the signs a short distance to Tropico.

Here is a gold discovery with a unique and inauspicious beginning. In 1878 Ezra Hamilton, owner of the East Side Pottery Company of Los Angeles, was searching for the right kind of potter's clay to use to make sewer pipe for the growing community of Los Angeles. He found this site to be so valuable that he bought the hill from its owner, Dr. L. A. Crandall, in 1882. In 1894, with the demand for his sewer pipe diminishing, Hamilton started to pan gold out of the clay. What he found made him forget all about the clay itself. By 1896 his gold operation, called the Lida Mine, was thriving. In 1908 Hamilton sold the Lida to the Tropico Mining and Milling Company, so named because many of the group of investors lived in the Los Angeles-area community of Tropico.

Clifford Burton, a Canadian who had made his first strike at Panamint (see Chapter Two), and his brother Cecil started out as employees of the Tropico Company and ended up the owners, and the mine eventually became known as Burton's Tropico Gold Mine. The enterprise prospered until World War I closed the mine in 1917. When President Roosevelt raised the price of gold from $20 to $35

Burton's Tropico Gold Mine, with residence and old Palmdale School in foreground

per ounce in the 1930s, the mine reopened, but it closed once more with the passage of Law 208 in 1942, which prohibited mining all but strategic materials during World War II. Some sporadic mining has been carried on since. Total production from Tropico has been estimated at between $6 million and $8 million.

In 1958 the Settle family began the project of reopening Tropico as a tourist attraction by bringing in structures from other mining camps and nearby towns, including the original Palmdale school. These buildings were placed at the foot of the southern slope of Tropico Hill, which makes for a dramatic photograph because the Tropico Mine is just above. But those same buildings were auctioned off in 1982 and will eventually be removed. Tours are given of the mine itself, including an impressive view 300 feet down a lighted shaft to the water that now fills the remaining 600 feet of the shaft. The museum adjacent to the mine tour has some fine historical photos and memorabilia.

Ghost town enthusiasts love to peer into the past. Well, residents of Kern County in A.D. 2866 will have a sterling opportunity to do just that at Trop-

ico. In 1966, the county's centennial year, a shaft containing artifacts of the present was sealed as a time tunnel to be opened at the celebration of Kern County's 1,000th anniversary.

WILLOW SPRINGS

Willow Springs is 5 miles west of the Tropico Gold Mine.

When his Lida Mine claim proved a winner, in 1900 Ezra Hamilton purchased the former stage stop at Willow Springs and 160 acres of surrounding land to ensure that the mill for his gold mine (see Tropico) would have sufficient water. He also began to envision another use for the shady site—as a resort for people suffering from lung diseases. It was an admirable plan, for Willow Springs is as pleasant and tranquil as Hamilton's mine must have been noisy, dirty, and dangerous. The resort opened in 1904, after Hamilton had spent $40,000 on the project. Eventually it would comprise twenty-seven stone buildings, including houses, a store, a garage, a generating plant, an icehouse, a hotel, a school, a public hall, a dance hall, a bathhouse, and a swim-

The headframe above Tropico looks down on the mine buildings.

Stone buildings of Hamilton's resort at Willow Springs

Deserted residence at Willow Springs

Area Four:
Near Lake Isabella

KEYESVILLE

The turnoff to Keyesville is one mile northwest of the town of Lake Isabella. Turn south opposite the Main Dam Campground and drive 2 miles down the paved Keyesville Road.

ming pool. Surrounding the resort were acres of vineyards, orchards, and mulberry trees.

Though Ezra Hamilton died in 1914, the resort did continue for a few years under Hamilton's son. But the post office closed in 1918, and the school became part of the Rosamond district in about 1927.

Willow Springs' dependable water had made it a frequently visited spot long before Ezra Hamilton. It was a campsite for Indians; Padre Garces and the Spanish came through in 1776; the John C. Fremont party stopped in 1844; the Jayhawker Party that narrowly escaped from Death Valley found water there in 1850; and in the 1860s, stagecoaches bound for Havilah and freight wagons heading for Cerro Gordo came across the Antelope Valley from Los Angeles and stopped at Willow Springs.

Today, over a dozen rock and adobe buildings, many of which are occupied, remain in Willow Springs, including the dance hall and the garage with its old gas pump.

Two other locations near Willow Springs and Tropico offer interesting remains. To see the head-frame and foundations of a mill at the Cactus Queen Mine, drive north from Willow Springs about 5.5 miles on Tehachapi-Willow Springs Road past Backus Road. The site stands right where the road takes a jog away from its due-north course. To view the remnants of the Elephant Eagle and the Golden Queen mines, return to Backus Road, drive east to Mojave-Tropico Road, and go north around Sole-dad Mountain onto Silver Queen Road. On your right you can see tailings, dumps, and evidence of mills and headframes.

Richard M. Keyes was a half-Indian veteran of the '49er Gold Rush who, in 1853, found gold in a quartz vein in what is now called Keyes Gulch; thus began the Kern River Gold Rush. The timing was perfect. The prosperity of the Gold Rush of 1849 was ending, and considerable financial panic existed in both San Francisco and the Gold Rush area. By the summer of 1855, more than 6,000 men were working the Kern River, most of them having arrived from '49er country. From 1853 until 1870, Keyesville (originally known as Hogeye) was the major placer and quartz gold-mining location in the Kern. It was incredibly isolated; for years it stood alone as the only supply point between Visalia, 110 miles to the northwest, and Los Angeles, 140 miles to the south.

When the post office opened in 1857, the population of about sixty patronized small wooden stores scattered in the valley and lived in tents and dirt-floored shacks in the hills above. The site was de-

Vacant wood-frame buildings at Keyesville

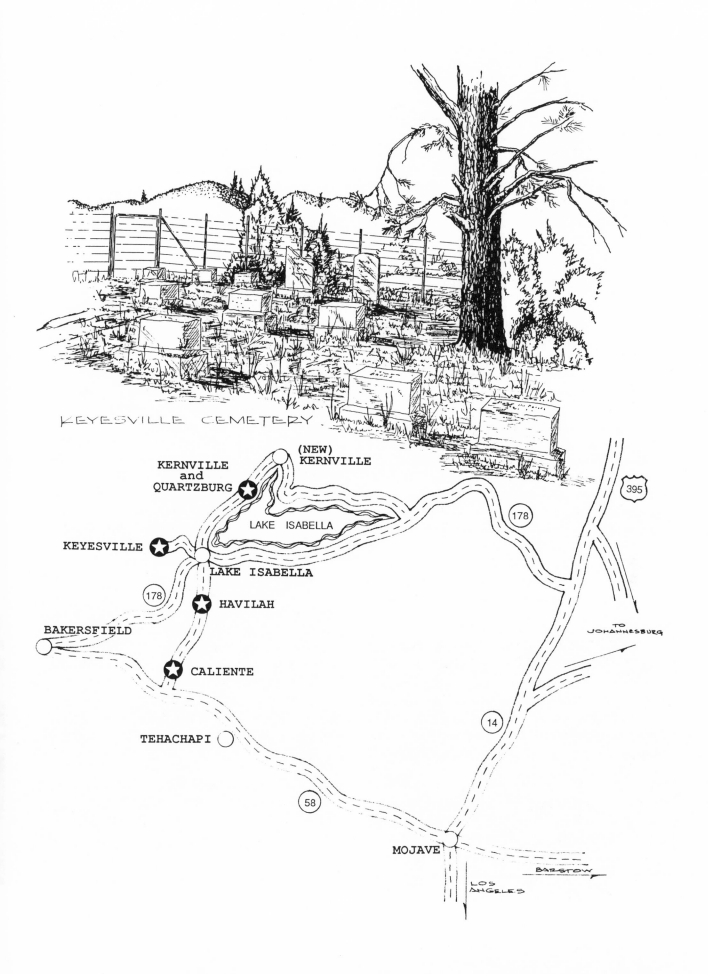

KEYESVILLE CEMETERY

(NEW)
KERNVILLE

KERNVILLE
and
QUARTZBURG

LAKE ISABELLA

KEYESVILLE

LAKE ISABELLA

178

178

HAVILAH

BAKERSFIELD

CALIENTE

395

TO JOHANNESBURG

14

TEHACHAPI

58

MOJAVE

BARSTOW

LOS ANGELES

scribed at the time as "not very imposing in appearance," despite its hotel, restaurant, and blacksmith shop. By the next year, five water-driven mills totaling twenty-two stamps were in operation. The population peaked during the Civil War, but in 1868 the post office was moved to Kernville (see following entry). Between 1897 and 1902 the post office was reopened as Keyes during a short resurrection of mining efforts. Further attempts were abandoned in 1915 and again in the 1930s. Total production from the two major mines in the district, the Keyes and the Mammoth, has been estimated at just under $1 million in gold and silver.

Keyesville today shows little evidence of its former importance to the Kern River Gold Rush. Seven buildings, three of them occupied, stand at the townsite, but almost certainly all date from the mining efforts undertaken in the '30s. They are clearly posted against trespassing. Across the road from them is a California Historical Landmark sign, behind which are the outlines of an interesting earthworks built in either 1856 or 1863 (sources disagree) in response to a threatened Indian attack that never materialized.

The Keyes Mill, with its ten stamps intact, stands .7 miles up a back road, but it is posted against trespassing: you should definitely request permission at the townsite before attempting to find it. But one more spot in Keyesville is not private, and it's worth investigating. Head back toward Lake Isabella for .4 miles, turn right where a fenced shaft is immediately to your left, and park your car or drive your four-wheel drive vehicle up the road .5 miles. A

The Keyesville cemetery

fenced-in cemetery stands there, near some large trees on your right.

Tombstones in cemeteries often pose more questions than they answer, but occasionally the stories are painfully clear. Here you will see the grave of the son of William and Frances Lightner, who lived for only three days in 1872. Next to him is his sister, who survived for three weeks in 1875. Then there is a double grave: the Lightners' son, who lived for seventeen days in 1876, and Frances Lightner herself, who died six days after giving birth to him.

KERNVILLE AND QUARTZBURG

The new community of Kernville is 11 miles north of the town of Lake Isabella. Old Kernville was about 1.2 miles north of Wofford Heights. Quartzburg was 1 mile north of old Kernville.

"Lovely" Rogers, a companion of Richard Keyes (see preceding entry), was furious. He had spent hours searching for a lost mule that had wandered from Keyesville. When he finally saw the beast, he picked up a rock to throw at it and found the specimen full of gold. That was in 1860. The camp that formed there was originally called Rogersville in honor of its founder, but within the first year the name was changed to Quartzburg, for the quartz-bearing gold. Rogers' discovery was the vein of what was to become the famous Big Blue Mine, which produced over $1.8 million in gold that was processed in an eighty-stamp mill capable of crushing 100 tons of rock per day. Next to the mill was a small community known as Burkeville for Edwin Burke, co-owner of the Big Blue. By 1876 the mine and mill were employing about two hundred men.

Quartzburg became a respectable town. Too respectable, in fact. A temperance movement in the town's first year turned Quartzburg dry, causing saloonkeeper Adam Hamilton to move one mile south. He is supposed to have placed a board across two whiskey barrels and announced that he was open for business. Quartzburg residents derisively dubbed Hamilton's new community Whiskey Flat, a name that stuck until 1864, when it became Kernville. Two years later, Kernville had residences and two or three saloons, hotels, and stores. In 1868 Kernville received its post office, transferred from Keyesville, with Adam Hamilton serving as the first postmaster.

The two rival towns became the center of the Kern River activity through the 1860s and 1870s, but when the Big Blue operations burned in 1883, the heyday of the two camps was over, although the mine remained at least somewhat active until 1907. Lake Isabella has now covered most of the original Kernville site. The present Kernville, to me the most pleasant of all the towns near Lake Isabella, was founded in 1951. The citizens of old Kernville were allowed to select a site out of the way of the lake to be formed. For the next two years, when the dam was to be finished, many of the best buildings in old Kernville, including motels, restaurants, stores, and homes, were moved to the new Kernville site. Although the original Kernville is under water, much of its flavor remains; the present Kernville is not, however, a ghost town in any sense of the word.

One item the Quartzburg and Kernville residents could agree upon was that a common cemetery should be located between the two towns. The Kern River Valley Cemetery is 1.5 miles north of Wofford Heights on the road to new Kernville. Turn right off the main road at the entrance to the campground to reach the cemetery's entrance. If you pass a new cemetery on your left while you are on the highway, you will have gone too far. Just north of the old cemetery, up the hill to your left, is what's left of the Big Blue Mine.

If you find maps as fascinating as I do, you'll enjoy comparing the topographic maps of the Lake Isabella area before and after the creation of the lake. Two old topos worth studying are the 1943 Isabella 15' and the 1956 Kernville 15'. The 1972 Lake Isabella 7½' map provides the contrast.

HAVILAH

Havilah is 7 miles south of Bodfish on the Caliente-Bodfish Road, which is an extension of Lake Isabella Boulevard.

Secessionist and Confederate sympathizer Asbury Harpending, a native of Kentucky, had helped to outfit a Confederate privateer in San Francisco in 1863, but the plot was discovered before the ship could depart. Harpending was put in jail for a few months; when he was released, he headed for the Kern River. With a few other Southern sympathizers he began mining along Clear Creek. Harpending called the settlement that developed in 1864 Havilah after the biblical land of gold mentioned in Genesis. Two years later the rush had reached almost biblical proportions with a horde of 3,000 miners living in the immediate area. Harpending discovered that you

Reconstructed Kern County Courthouse at Havilah

don't have to be a miner to find gold: he laid out the town, sold lots for $20 a front foot, and left in 1865 to return to San Francisco with about $800,000.

By early 1866 Havilah—comprised principally of Americans, Mexicans, Frenchmen, and Chinese—featured 147 buildings, including a bakery, thirteen saloons, gambling halls, dance halls, brothels, a blacksmith shop, hotels, billiard parlors, a Catholic church, and ten operating mills. The principal producers were the Joe Walker Mine and the Delphi (also known as the McKneadney) Mine.

When Kern County was formed in April 1866, Havilah was chosen as county seat, so the town added a courthouse, jail, and school. Four months later the first edition of the *Havilah Courier* hit the streets, with strong political leanings: "County Clerk has opened the Great Register, and the editor hopes that every Democrat will immediately enroll himself as a voter."

Alan Hensher and Jack Peskin, in their informative booklet *Ghost Towns of the Kern and the Eastern Sierra,* relate one observer's reaction to Havilah at its peak: "If ever there was a God-forsaken set of reprobates collected in an unprotected town in the states, it is here. . . . From morning to night, and night to morning, it is one ceaseless round of drinking and gambling, only varied by an occasional shooting scrape or fight." One wonders what his assessment would be of present-day Las Vegas.

Only one-quarter of the mills were still in operation by 1867, and the mines played out for good in 1869; by the time the nationwide depression of 1873 hit, Havilah was moribund. The county seat had been moved to Bakersfield in 1872, and the Joe Walker Mine shut down in 1874 due to flooding. The post office closed in 1918, followed in a year by the public school.

When you enter Havilah from the north, the first major building you'll see will be the dark brown wooden courthouse, a 1968 replica of the one built in 1866. Nearby is a reconstruction of the 1867 schoolhouse. Farther south on the same side of the street, partially hidden behind some alianthus, stands the stone ruin of the Havilah Commercial Company. On the south end of town is a small cemetery.

CALIENTE

Caliente is 23 miles south of Havilah.

Gabriel Allen founded Allen's Camp as a place to transfer his merchandise—brought from Los An-geles—from more economical wagons to more ma-neuverable pack teams that could carry supplies on the poor roads and trails leading to Kern River gold camps like Havilah.

By the time Southern Pacific railroad crews ar-rived to build a rail link between Los Angeles and San Francisco in the mid-1870s, Allen's Camp was little more than a deserted cabin near a brackish spring. The first train arrived in April 1875, estab-lishing a community that was to be home for some 200 permanent residents and 2,000 workers, princi-pally Chinese, as they aimed the route toward the summit of Tehachapi Pass. The Southern Pacific route was stalled at Caliente for almost a year as construction gangs took on what was to become a legendary engineering feat—the grade to Tehach-api Pass.

The post office was established in 1875, using the Southern Pacific's choice of names—Caliente—since the community was near Agua Caliente Creek; Allen's Camp was a name relegated to historical footnote. Caliente became a shipping center for the

The tiny Caliente cemetery, with townsite and tracks beyond

cattle ranches nearby and for freight heading to and from Cerro Gordo and the Kern River gold camps, although by that time the Kern River Rush was fading considerably. The year 1875 was Caliente's only great year, however. The south side of the street along the railroad tracks featured all the usual businesses (several general stores, three hotels, two drugstores, more than a dozen restaurants), while the north side contained solely saloons, over twenty in number.

The Tehachapi Pass project was a staggering undertaking. The tracks had to rise three thousand feet from Caliente to Tehachapi, only sixteen air miles distant, without exceeding a 2.2-percent grade. The ascent began with a wide horseshoe arc out of Caliente and culminated at the now-famous Tehachapi Loop, where the grade rose 587 feet in only five miles as the track made a complete loop over itself. After crossing the pass in July 1876, the route was finished in under three months. The 478-mile link between Los Angeles and San Francisco was complete.

After the railroad crossed Tehachapi Pass, the construction population moved on, and many of the businesses were moved to Bakersfield. Caliente was still significant to the Southern Pacific as a water stop for locomotives, however, as well as the switching site where extra locomotives were added for the difficult pull over Tehachapi Pass. But the days of glory, and they were few, were over for Caliente by 1877.

Today Caliente is more of a "place where" kind of ghost town. It doesn't resemble a thriving railroad camp, and not much of antiquity remains. Only three structures are vacant among several occupied buildings. A tiny cemetery stands on a low hill just north of town. From there you can get a good view of the train activity around Tehachapi Pass. And that is what I like about Caliente. One can stand on a hill and envision, at least a bit, what this now-peaceful valley must have looked like with over 2,000 people pushing progress up the hill.

Capsule Summary

MAJOR SITES

Randsburg—good main street, mining evidence
Calico—a few authentic structures and a cemetery in a tourist town
Llano—foundations, walls, lime kilns

SECONDARY SITES

Providence—walls, foundations, mining remains in a memorable setting
Tropico—buildings, memorabilia, mine tour
Kelso—excellent depot in a small town
Ludlow—remnants from two eras
Garlock—photogenic buildings and arrastre
Red Mountain—commercial buildings, school, Kelly Mine
Willow Springs—several good adobe buildings
Havilah—walls, foundations, reconstructed buildings

MINOR SITES

Ivanpah—scattered walls, foundations, debris
Keyesville—mill and residences on private property; cemetery
Johannesburg—interesting cemetery in active town
Atolia—buildings, mine evidence
Goler—foundations of a mill
Stedman—mining evidence
Caliente—small cemetery
Silver Lake—one desolate building
Ragtown—faint foundations, mining evidence
Quartzburg—remains of a mine
(Old) Kernville—cemetery

ROAD CONDITIONS

Ragtown, Stedman, Ivanpah, Goler—unpaved roads suitable for passenger cars
Providence—unpaved truck road
All other sites—paved roads

TRIP SUGGESTIONS

TRIP 1: Calico, Ludlow, Ragtown, Stedman, Kelso, Providence, Ivanpah, Silver Lake. This long loop from Barstow might possibly be accomplished in one very long day, but I'd recommend two more leisurely paced days. This would be an excellent trip for a camp-out. Total round-trip distance from Barstow, approximately 360 miles.

TRIP 2: Llano, Tropico, Willow Springs. These sites are easily visited as side trips on a journey from the Los Angeles area to Mojave, about 100 miles to the northeast. Visiting these sites would add about 65 miles.

TRIP 3: Randsburg Area. You could visit all the sites in this vicinity in a one-day trip from either Mo-

jave or Barstow. Round-trip distance from Mojave, 95 miles; from Barstow, 160 miles.

TRIP 4: Keyesville, (Old) Kernville, Quartzburg,
Havilah, and Caliente. All the sites in the Lake
Isabella area can be visited on a full day's outing
from Bakersfield. Round-trip mileage, about 140
miles.

TRIP 5: Combine trip suggestions in this chapter
with those in other chapters: Trip 1, above, could
be altered to head north from Baker to Death Valley (Chapter Two); and the Lake Isabella (Trip 4)
and Randsburg (Trip 3) sites could be combined
with those in Inyo County (Chapter One) or
Death Valley (Chapter Two).

TOPOGRAPHIC MAP INFORMATION FOR CHAPTER THREE:
GHOSTS OF THE MOJAVE AND THE KERN
(For map-reading assistance, consult Appendix A.)

Site	Topo Map Name	Size	Year	Importance*
Calico	Yermo	7½'	1953 (pr[a] 1970)	3
Ludlow	Ludlow	7½'	1955	3
Ragtown	Ludlow	7½'	1955	2
Stedman	Ludlow	7½'	1955	2
	Morgans Well	7½'	1955	3
Kelso	Kelso	7½'	1983 prv[b]	3
Providence	Fountain Peak	7½'	1985	2
	Colton Well	7½'	1984	2
Silver Lake	Baker	7½'	1983	3
Ivanpah	Clark Mountain	7½'	1985	2
	Ivanpah Lake	7½'	1985	3
	Mineral Hill	7½'	1983	3
Goler	Garlock	7½'	1967	2
	El Paso Peaks	7½'	1967	2
Randsburg	Johannesburg	7½'	1967	2
Garlock	Garlock	7½'	1967	3
Johannesburg	Johannesburg	7½'	1967	3
Atolia	Red Mountain	7½'	1967	3
Red Mountain	Red Mountain	7½'	1967	3
Llano	Lovejoy Buttes	7½'	1957 (pr[a] 1974)	3
	Valyermo	7½'	1958 (pr[a] 1974)	2
Tropico	Rosamond	7½'	1973	3
	Soledad Mountain	7½'	1973	3
Willow Springs	Willow Springs	7½'	1965 (pr[a] 1974)	3
Keyesville	Alta Sierra	7½'	1972	2
Kernville (Old)	Lake Isabella North	7½'	1972 (pr[a] 1985)	2
Quartzburg	Lake Isabella North	7½'	1972 (pr[a] 1985)	2
Havilah	Miracle Hot Springs	7½'	1972	3
Caliente	Bena	7½'	1972	3
	Oiler Peak	7½'	1972	3

[a]—photo revised (see Appendix A, "Distinguishing Characteristics")
[b]—provisional edition (see Appendix A, "Distinguishing Characteristics")

*1—essential to find and/or enjoy site to fullest
 2—helpful but not essential
 3—unnecessary to find and enjoy site

4. Ghost Towns of the Southland

This is a chapter for those who crave the solitude that the Los Angeles and San Diego areas seem to hide so cleverly.

The sites that follow are, with the exception of one (Julian), ghost towns for loners—you can count on few people and lots of space. All encourage you to get out of your vehicle and explore the surroundings; in fact, you cannot even see much without taking pleasant strolls. Nevertheless, all of the sites but one (Picacho) stand either along a paved road or within a short drive of one, so you can achieve that sought-after isolation without having to disappear completely into the hills.

You will also discover variety in this chapter. Five of the sites, like so many others in this book, are gold-mine locations. But you'll also visit a couple of stage stations, some almost forgotten cemeteries, an aqueduct ghost town, a townsite bisected by a canal, a company town that's now a prison, a ghost island, and even a ghost road.

Area One: East of Los Angeles

HOLCOMB VALLEY
(BELLEVILLE AND DOBLE)

Holcomb Valley is north of Big Bear Lake, which is about 45 miles northeast of San Bernardino. Take state routes 330 or 18 to Fawnskin and points east.

William Francis "Bill" Holcomb left Indiana for the California goldfields in 1850 and found great frustration but little gold. In 1859 he forsook the Gold Rush country and headed for the Southland. While employed as a hunter in Bear Valley, Holcomb discovered what became one of Southern California's richest goldfields on May 5, 1860. Two months later, Holcomb Valley was crowded with prospectors who were finding gold both in placers and in quartz-bearing deposits. The initial activity ended in the 1880s, but some mining continued as late as the 1950s.

Bear Valley, at an elevation of 6,700 feet, is now popular as a cool summer retreat and a winter ski

Log cabin at Belleville in Holcomb Valley

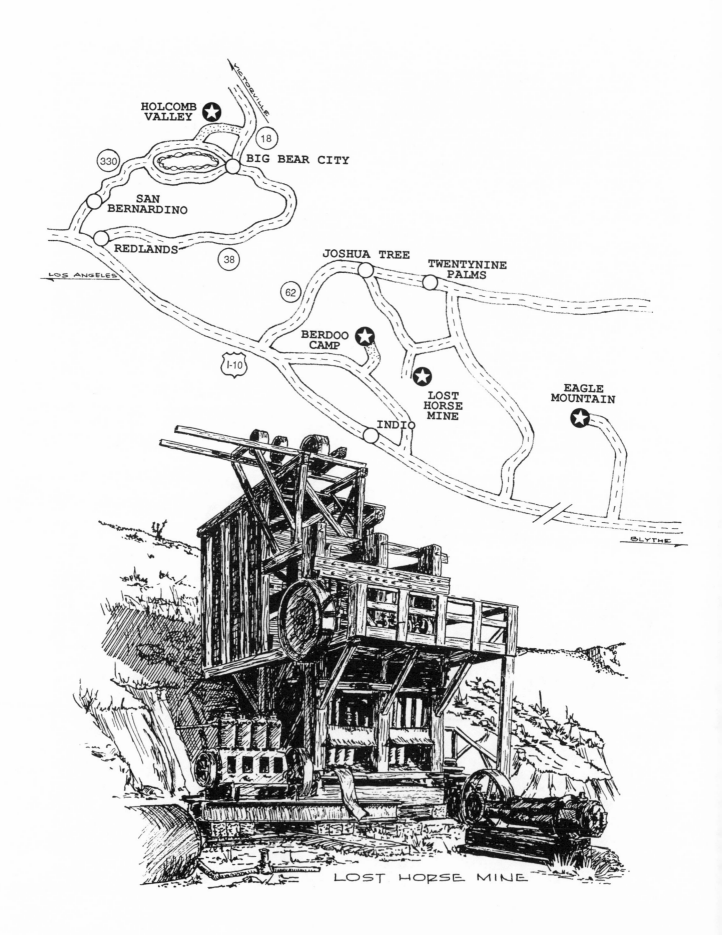

LOST HORSE MINE

Holcomb Valley's "Pygmy Cabin"; the doorway is 4½ feet tall. This photo was taken in 1984, but a visit in 1988 found it burned to the ground.

area. But considerable evidence of the mining fury remains—if you know where to look. And the Big Bear Ranger Station, on the north side of Big Bear Lake on state route 38, has produced an excellent brochure as a guide. Their loop drive covers just over 12 miles and gives you all the points of interest along the way, except for one that I will add. One of the best features of the ranger station's "Gold Fever Trail Self-Guided Tour" is that it will require you to take several short walks out of your car and into the splendid countryside that is Holcomb Valley.

Along this route you will visit, among other stops, the sites of the two principal Holcomb Valley towns, Belleville and Doble. Belleville, which almost became the county seat during its heyday, was named for Belle, the daughter of Jed Van Dusen, blacksmith and road builder. His wife was supposed to have made a flag out of petticoats for the town's first Fourth of July celebration. Belleville, which once boasted a stamp mill, saloons, a butcher shop, and a sawmill, today features one cabin—still under

roof—and an arrastre. Evidence abounds of the placer diggings nearby. Just under a mile away are the remains of the log building that was once Two Gun Bill's Saloon.

Also in the area may be a reconstruction of the so-called "pygmy cabin," a tiny structure that at one time in the 1930s served as a barbershop. I say "may be" because I photographed it in 1984, but on a second visit, in 1988, I found the pygmy cabin had been burned to the ground. The original restoration of the cabin had been an Eagle Boy Scout project of Michael Sean Henderson, and a remarkably thoughtless person destroyed that worthwhile effort. But I sincerely hope that someone else will build another cabin for others to enjoy.

On the east end of the self-guided tour is a stop at the mill near Gold Mountain. The Gold Mountain Mine was owned by E. J. "Lucky" Baldwin, who had made a fortune in the Comstock Lode. Baldwin operated the mine from about 1860 to 1900, and later owners worked it on an intermittent basis into

Hopper of the mill of the Gold Mountain Mine in Holcomb Valley; Baldwin Lake is at upper right.

the 1940s. Remnants of the forty-stamp mill and cyanide-processing plant, which date from the 1870s, command a dramatic view of Baldwin Lake and the surrounding valley.

Not mentioned in the self-guided tour is the now-vanished community of Doble, named for Baldwin's son-in-law, Budd Doble. Only a few slight unnatural hillocks hint that man was ever there, but the nearby cemetery remains. About one-quarter of a mile before you reach the paved road that completes your tour, you will see, behind a fence, a faint road heading north for just a short way and some recently placed crosses that are visible from your road.

The ranger station brochure, which is interesting and informative in all respects, goes into much more detail than I have; I've merely highlighted the spots that interested me the most, since to duplicate the brochure would be superfluous. Plan on at least three hours for the loop—and take along a picnic lunch for maximum enjoyment.

BERDOO CAMP

Berdoo Camp is near Indio. See the text for detailed directions.

The Colorado River Aqueduct, which brings water from Parker Dam to Los Angeles, in some ways brought urbanization to the desert. The project began in 1923 with a study, planning, and financing period that took until 1932, when construction actually began. It was completed on October 14, 1939, but not before over 35,000 people worked on the enormous undertaking, creating 92 miles of tunnels, 63 miles of concrete-lined canals, 55 miles of concrete conduits, three dams, five pumping plants, 237 miles of high-voltage electric-power transmission lines, and countless miles of roads—many of which became public thoroughfares.

The project was sectioned into camps where men, equipment, and supplies were centralized. Four of these camps were "division headquarters"—larger, more completely equipped towns. The first was at Parker Dam on the Colorado River, the next at Iron Mountain, the third near Eagle Mountain (see entry, Chapter 4), and the last at Berdoo Camp, near Indio. Berdoo Camp is the one to visit—an aqueduct ghost town. It was the division headquarters of the East Coachella Tunnel, an 18.3-mile link in the remarkable construction project.

Berdoo Camp was born in early 1933; a waterline reached the site in April of that year, and a telephone switchboard (part of a $260,000 phone system that connected the camps) was in place by July. The camp buildings were primarily wood frame with plasterboard or fiberboard walls. Two-story dormitories held two workers per room; a fully equipped kitchen served hearty meals (a camp reported that the consumption of turkey one Thanksgiving was five pounds per man). The men who lived in the dormitories were charged $1.15 for meals and $.25 for lodging per day. Workers could also spend their money at the half-wood, half-canvas camp store, which one visitor said sold everything from clothing to tobacco.

The centerpiece of Berdoo Camp was an air-conditioned, twelve-bed hospital (raised to twenty-seven and finally thirty-five beds as construction crews increased in number). The hospital was supervised by a surgeon of "outstanding industrial and orthopedic experience," according to a 1935 Metropolitan Water District (M.W.D.) publication,

Part of the foundations and walls at Berdoo Camp

and the hospital featured X-ray equipment, a modern operating room, and all the necessary instruments. The publication went on to say, "Many remarkable surgical operations have been accomplished here."

A photograph of Berdoo Camp from an M.W.D. report published in 1935 shows more than thirty-five identifiable buildings, most lining the main street that rises from a trestle over a wash up onto the sloping foothill on which the townsite rests.

When the Coachella construction work was completed in 1937, much of the equipment and all camp buildings were put up for sale. The hospital had closed in October 1936 as construction in the immediate area of Berdoo Camp was completed. A 1939 publication of the M.W.D. states that the hospital had handled 12,000 admissions, including 3,000 actual hospitalizations. That number is impressively low. Safety precautions were considerable for that time and accident rates were well below those for any tunneling project to that date, according to the M.W.D., which announced " . . . that construction hazards can be overcome and that high construction speeds can be obtained without sacrifice of human life and limb."

The Berdoo Camp of today certainly shows that it was a company town: the many foundations, walls, steps, and ramps are all poured concrete, and the site gives evidence of a definite master plan as opposed to the fairly random growth of boomtowns. No real

Concrete walls of Berdoo Camp

buildings remain, a testimony to the impermanence of the camp and the thoroughness of the salvage. The paved road into Berdoo Camp would still be drivable but for the destruction of it near the entrance in the canyon, where once there was a trestle. In fact, the main stretch through town is in considerably better shape than some rural roads presently being "maintained" in California. The excellent desert view from Berdoo Camp, at an elevation of almost 1,800 feet, down to the Coachella Valley (at sea level and below) and across to the Santa Rosa Range is a most agreeable addition to an already interesting site.

You cannot see the aqueduct at the townsite, as it is, of course, a tunnel in the mountains. When Berdoo Camp was in operation, the workers had to enter an adit near camp that went underground for 2,042 feet into the mountain before even reaching the tunnel itself. The tunnel distance excavated by the Berdoo Camp work crews was 29,101 feet—just over 5.5 miles—the greatest distance accomplished by any of the camps.

Although *California Place Names* does not have an entry for Berdoo Camp in Berdoo Canyon in the Little San Bernardino Mountains, it does provide an interesting etymological footnote to the site. San Berdoo, as most Southern Californians know, is a familiar but vaguely disparaging name for San Bernardino. Berdoo Canyon was named, no doubt, by some cartographers with a sense of humor, since names of other hills and canyons in the proximity are whimsical variations upon San Bernardino: Bern, Bernard, Berdoo, Dino, North Dino, Little Berdoo, and Round Berdoo.

To visit Berdoo Camp, take the first Interstate 10 exit east of Indio onto Dillon Road, which is shown on most highway maps as the route that swings around behind Indio and goes up to the town of Desert Hot Springs. Go 6.3 miles north-northwest on Dillon Road and turn northeast on a paved road heading into the mountains. The pavement ends in about 1.3 miles; from there a dirt road with occasional patches of pavement continues. You will proceed a total of 3.2 miles from the intersection with Dillon Road. In a canyon, a dirt road will swing steeply up to your left; park your car and take about a five-minute walk to the townsite. The road is not passable. The 1958 Lost Horse Mountain 15′ topographic map is helpful in finding Berdoo Camp. The road you will take in is marked on the map as going into Berdoo Canyon, and the townsite is near the spot on the map at which the Colorado River

Aqueduct passes close to a marked mine dump.

(Note: Along Dillon Road, heading northwest toward Desert Hot Springs, are many small abandoned houses along with some that are occupied.)

LOST HORSE MINE

Within the boundaries of the Joshua Tree National Monument, Lost Horse Mine is 23 miles southwest of the Oasis Visitor Center in Twentynine Palms, or about 20 miles from the town of Joshua Tree. Follow the signs toward Keys View overlook; on the way is the clearly marked turnoff to Lost Horse Mine. The 1.5-mile hike to the site will probably take you about thirty to forty minutes. Plan on spending around two hours for the hike and visit.

A hawk could fly from Berdoo Camp to Lost Horse Mine in fewer than 8 miles. You, alas, will have to drive about 65 miles if you want to stay on paved roads. The dirt road through Berdoo Canyon that got you up to the turnoff to Berdoo Camp does cross the Little San Bernardino Mountains and come down into Pleasant Valley within Joshua Tree National Monument, but I can only say that the road deteriorated markedly as I headed into the canyon beyond the turnoff to Berdoo Camp. I turned back because my map, the 1958 Lost Horse Mountain topo, designated the road a jeep trail; however, the brochure available at Joshua Tree National Monument headquarters, which I visited later in the day, shows the road as a "dirt road."

The Lost Horse is a mine that the dedicated ghost town hunter must not miss. First, it's in some of the most beautiful high desert in the West. Second, the walk to the site is exhilarating and photogenic (especially photogenic in the late afternoon). And, finally, the Lost Horse Mine has one of the best examples that I have ever seen of a ten-stamp mill that remains at its original location (as opposed, say, to one in a museum). It has escaped much of the looting and vandalism that, sadly, is so common with other mills, because it stands in a national monument.

The wooden mill with its iron stamps, the belts, the remnants of two diesel engines, and two large tanks sit on the western slope of Lost Horse Mountain at an altitude of 5,000 feet; Joshua trees, thick at the trail head, thin out at the foot of the mountain, and scrub desert vegetation predominates.

Lost Horse Mine received its name, according to Ronald Dean Miller in *Mines of the High Desert,* because in 1893 "Dutch Frank" Diebold, Ed

Ten-stamp mill of the Lost Horse Mine

Holland, and Alfred G. Tingman were camped in the area and had their horses stolen. Diebold found the horses the next day at the camp of the locally notorious McHaney gang, where armed toughs informed Diebold, "You did not lose any horses." When Diebold attempted to describe the "lost" animals, he was cut short by McHaney, this time in a more ominous tone: "Remember, you didn't lose no horses." Diebold replied, "No, I guess I didn't."

The "lost"-horse story then takes a decidedly better turn. On his trip back to camp, Diebold found a rich gold vein. He eventually sold his claim, named, appropriately, the Lost Horse, to Johnny Lang, a saloon keeper near Twentynine Palms Oasis, for $1,000. Lang took in as partners the other two men of the lost-horse escapade, Holland and Tingman. The three were reported to have made $3,000 each by the end of one month's efforts.

Eventually Jep Ryan, from Banning, bought out Holland and Tingman. Ryan suspected his new partner, Lang, of mischief when he recognized a disturbing pattern in the operations: the size of the

amalgam ball from his day-shift operations was consistently larger than Lang's night-shift efforts. Ryan had a man watch Lang, and his misgivings were substantiated; Johnny Lang was highgrading his own mine. Lang, confronted with the evidence, was forced to sell out for $12,000.

Lang lived in the nearby hills thereafter, doing some modest prospecting. In January 1925 a note was found attached to his shack saying, "Gone for grub." Several months later, his nearly mummified remains were found; nearby were a square inch of bacon and a trace of flour. Johnny Lang, age seventy-three, was wrapped in canvas and buried at the site of his death.

One other site may be available for you to visit. The Desert Queen Ranch, operated by Bill Keys (see Death Valley Ranch entry) from 1909 until his death in 1969, is open occasionally for tours led by the Joshua Tree Natural History Society. I know of this only by report, as the tours were not operating when I visited Joshua Tree. The one-hour visit, for which there is a nominal charge, takes you through

Looking down at the Lost Horse Mine and Joshua Tree National Monument; part of the trail to the site is visible.

Keys's ranch, which looks as if it had just recently been deserted. Bill Keys scavenged from abandoned mines and ranches and also constructed creative ways of coping with the desert—like dams to trap runoff rainwater and irrigation pipes to nourish crops. The ranch is on an access road behind a locked gate near Hidden Valley Campground. The road out to Lost Horse Mine continues to Keys View, named for Bill Keys, who constructed part of the original road himself as a route to his Hidden Gold Mine, also known as the Desert Queen Mine. From Keys View you can see a truly remarkable panorama of the Indio area far below.

To check on the availability of tours of the Desert Queen Ranch, write: Superintendent, Joshua Tree National Monument, 74485 National Monument Drive, Twentynine Palms, CA 92277 or call ahead (619-367–7511).

EAGLE MOUNTAIN

Eagle Mountain is 13 miles north of Desert Center on county road R2. Desert Center is 46 miles east of Indio and 46 miles west of Blythe on I-10.

Mining towns of the modern era tend to disappear completely. They are company towns owned by corporations that realize the transitory nature of the business, so they tend to put up nondescript residences or use mobile homes for employees and build even mills and smelters so that they can be dismantled. One can hardly be critical of such a practice, as it is fiscally responsible. But the sad fact is that, as a result of this frugality, people of the

Eagle Mountain's movie theater and parking lot

twenty-first century are going to see very little evidence of the ghost towns of the 1940s and beyond.

So what a pleasant surprise is Eagle Mountain. Once home to several hundred people, here is a complete town—dozens of residences, a movie theater, two schools, a market, a launderette, a church, a doctor's and dentist's offices, company headquarters, and a workable mine—all in restorable shape. And restored it will be, as Eagle Mountain is to be put to use in one of the most practical utilizations imaginable for a deserted, isolated town—as a minimum-

A portion of the shopping center at Eagle Mountain

Residential area at Eagle Mountain

Company housing—Eagle Mountain

security prison leased from the site's owner, Kaiser Steel.

Two of the early claims in the Eagle Mountains, developed sometime before the turn of the century, were the Iron Chief and the Iron Eagle. In the early 1900s, a miner named Dofflemeyer and two partners were working the Iron Chief claim for gold but were finding the going very rough because of hard magnetic clumps they called "iron spuds" that were ruining their five-stamp mill. The real value of those spuds was recognized by E. H. Harriman, who bought out the claims and found himself the owner, as author Ronald Dean Miller put it, of a mountain of iron, some of the original claims assaying at fifty-four percent pure.

Even so, the 1943 topographic maps of the area show scant mining evidence; actually, the most prominent feature is the Eagle Mountain Aqueduct Station, a division headquarters and pumping plant for the Colorado River Aqueduct that had been completed only four years earlier (see Berdoo Camp entry for more on the aqueduct project). But during World War II the demand for iron brought about increased mining activity in the vicinity; the 1956 ore production was reported at 2,650,000 tons, with smaller claims long having been consolidated into the Eagle Mountain Mine by Kaiser Steel.

So what will be in store for you? I visited Eagle Mountain in the spring of 1988, two months before the first prisoners were due to arrive. I was given a thorough tour of the site by Larry Charpied, a security official. He explained that when the mine closed in 1983 there was considerable bitterness both in Eagle Mountain and nearby Desert Center; as a result, the citizens of the area are quite enthusiastic about the opening of the prison. The Lake Tamarisk subdivision, for example, has fallen on depressed times, and residents are hoping that the planned community and golf course, built by Kaiser Steel for its upper-management employees, can be maintained by inmate labor. In addition, security and support personnel will increase the population of the communities, perhaps bringing back services that are now lacking, such as a doctor and a dentist, as well as opening up possible employment opportunities for local residents.

On the road from Desert Center heading north to Eagle Mountain you will be crossing over terrain that General George Patton used in preparation for his North Africa campaign (and where, for years, people have scoured the desert with metal detectors looking for shell casings). You'll also see the Eagle Mountain Pumping Plant, and one other unusual sight—a string of garages in the middle of the desert. I was told that Kaiser Steel sold off about fifty houses at Eagle Mountain, and the buyer was given a deadline for their removal. As the time approached, he found that all he could remove with his equipment were the garages; so there they stand, waiting for a fleet of nonexistent automobiles.

Naturally, security procedures will likely affect your ability to see the town, although even if you can't enter the site itself you can still see quite a bit from the road. When I was there, for example, the public school was outside a fence and the marked "no trespassing" signs, and a portion of the residential area could be photographed from there. Whatever the arrangements are when you read this, you can certainly appreciate the need to respect the prison's regulations concerning visiting the site.

Finally, it is very possible that the prison won't be there at all in a few years. A considerable ore body still exists, and eventually, given the right set of variables, Kaiser Steel will likely reopen the Eagle Mountain Mine. A U.S. Bureau of Mines study shows that the claims could daily supply a plant with a capacity of a thousand tons of pig iron for a hundred years.

Area Two: East of San Diego

Visitors to the San Diego area who hurry across the desert or hug the coastline on the wide, characterless freeways miss some of the most historically interesting and beautifully varied countryside in Southern California. And among this scenery one can discover ranchos, abandoned mines, stage stations, and ghost towns. A good source book for this area is *Mines of Julian,* by Helen Ellsberg (see Bibliography).

JULIAN

Julian is about 60 miles northeast of San Diego. Take Interstate 8 east and turn north on state route 79.

The Julian area came to life in 1869 when A. E. "Fred" Coleman discovered placer gold in a creek. Coleman founded the Coleman Mining District; the camp that developed there was called Emily City. In November of the same year, Drury and James Bailey arrived in the vicinity along with their cousins, Mike and Webb Julian. The four were Civil War veterans from Georgia who, discouraged with the conditions of the South during the carpetbagger era, had resolved to move west. In February 1870, Drury Bailey and Mike Julian formed the Julian Mining District after discovering a quartz deposit that they mined under the name of the Warrior's Rest. Within the week, three other mines opened.

The first strike of any real importance was the George Washington, due north of the present townsite. It was so named because H. C. Bickers, who found the gold-bearing quartz, tried to show the find to his two companions, but one was a preacher, and as it was Sunday, he refused to examine it. He did, however, look on Monday, which was February 22, 1870.

A town was laid out in 1870 by Bailey on land that he owned and named for his cousin, Mike. Bailey said that he thought Julian was a better-sounding name for a town than Bailey, and Julian was a family name anyway. Julian became popular with Southerners who had headed west after the Civil War. Since both the Julian and Bailey families were from Georgia, the hospitality of the town was

in marked contrast to San Diego, for example, where Alonzo Horton, the "Father of San Diego," was openly hostile to "rebels." This anti-Confederate feeling eventually kept some Northern capitalists from giving financial backing to the Julian mines.

The population soared to 800 within months as gold seekers poured in and created a tent city, with lots selling for between $50 and $150. In August of the same year a post office was established. Other camps sprang up as well: Emily City had become Coleman City, to the west of Julian was Eastwood, and to the east, Branson City. The biggest gold strike occurred in March 1870, when the Stonewall Jackson Mine was discovered south of Julian (see entry, Chapter 4).

Julian became a thriving town in the 1870s. Along with the usual saloons and dance halls there were five stores, two restaurants, and two hotels, as well as other businesses.

The first excitement was over by 1876 and the population dropped to about a hundred. Many of the miners who did stay on into the 1880s eventually deserted Julian to head for the silver mines of Tombstone, Arizona. But the discovery of the Gold King and Gold Queen mines in 1888, along with the resurrection of the nearby Stonewall Mine in the late 1880s, brought renewed interest in the Julian mines, and by 1896 Julian's population topped 1,000.

By this time Julian was also becoming known for a commodity that was much less transitory than mining—agriculture. James Madison had purchased a shipment of young apple trees and found that the climate, soil, and availability of water made Julian a natural food basket for grains and fruits. Arthur Juch, who came to Julian to install mining machinery in the Owens Mine, opted to work above ground and became well known as "Julian's Apple King." Today, with mining apparently dead, people still come to Julian to sample the area's world-famous apples.

Mining in this second period lasted near Julian until about the turn of the century, and other attempts were undertaken in the 1920s and '30s. The total production of gold has been estimated at about $7 million.

The gold from the ground might be gone, but not the gold to be found in the pockets of tourists. Julian has become a favorite stop for San Diegans looking for a pleasant retreat. Main Street features crafts shops and comfortable restaurants catering to

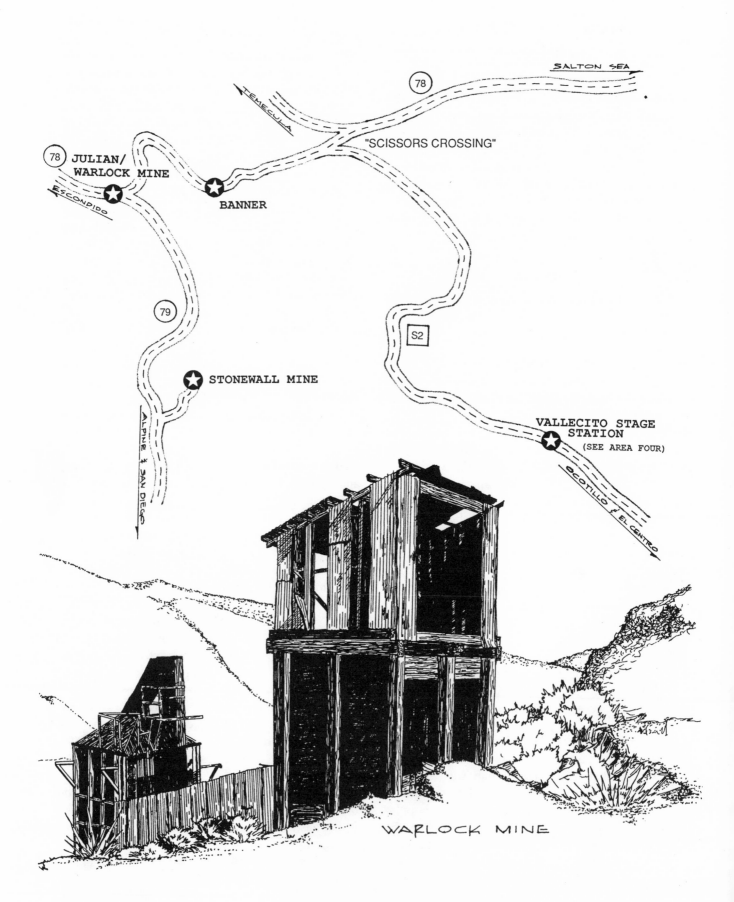

SALTON SEA

78

TEMECULA

"SCISSORS CROSSING"

78 JULIAN/
WARLOCK MINE

ESCONDIDO

BANNER

79

STONEWALL MINE

ALPINE & SAN DIEGO

S2

VALLECITO STAGE
STATION
(SEE AREA FOUR)

OCOTILLO & EL CENTRO

WARLOCK MINE

Main Street in Julian

vacationers, while a mercantile, a hardware store, and other shops trade principally with residents. Several structures among the modern activity of Julian remind the visitor of its earlier days: the historic, luxurious Julian Hotel, the oldest hotel in continuous service in San Diego County; the Wilcox Building, erected in 1871, on Main Street; the austere, two-cell jail, at the corner of 4th and "C" streets; and the wonderful, improbable library, formerly the Santa Ysabel School at nearby Witch Creek, which was moved to Julian and now stands at the corner of 4th and Washington.

You can get an excellent overview of Julian from the attractive and interesting cemetery, the entrance to which is at Main and "A" Streets. Drury Bailey, founding father of Julian, died in 1921; he is buried there next to his wife. South of town runs Coleman Creek, named for the man whose discovery started it all.

Interested in an outstanding hike from Julian?

Julian Jail at 4th and "C" streets

Drive east out of town on state route 78 for about a mile and turn right on Whispering Pines Road. Take an immediate right onto Woodland Road. After about a half a mile of uphill driving you will come to an even spot where the smooth pavement ends. The road forks just ahead of you. You can either park here or drive a bit father, depending upon your vehicle. You'll go down into a small ravine. The trail that heads down the northern slope of the mountains is the old Banner Grade (the "new" Banner Grade is highway 78, which goes through what's left of Banner on its way to the Salton Sea). This old road is now definitely a trail, with washouts making even four-wheel drive travel impossible. Down the old grade 1.5 miles is the Warlock Mine—deserted, dilapidated, delightful. The hike will take you about forty minutes under normal conditions (that is an estimate; I was trudging through eighteen-inch snowdrifts on my visit), and you will descend about 700 feet in elevation, so be prepared for a stiffer return trip.

But the Warlock Mine is worth it (and besides, the scenery is wonderful). Four buildings of the corrugated-tin variety stand at the Warlock, all under roof at this writing. The most interesting is the ball mill, with its complicated apparatus rusting in the semidarkness. The most remarkable feature is a small house trailer inside one of the buildings. Getting that abode to the Warlock Mine was no small feat. The entire site has been subjected to considerable vandalism, which is especially evident if you look at photographs of the site from books written in the last twenty years. Naturally, you know that this historic site should be respected and preserved.

Incidentally, beyond the Warlock Mine, which stands about halfway down the old Banner Grade, is private property. The road comes out at the locked gate mentioned in the next entry. Plan on spending

Remnants of the conveyor and mill at the Warlock Mine

Two of the Warlock Mine's buildings; a small house trailer is inside the shed on the left.

two to three hours on the Warlock Mine hike. The Julian 7½′ topographic map helps you get a clearer picture of the hike and the various locations of mines in the vicinity.

The Warlock Mine has had one of the longest lives of all the mines in the Julian-Banner District. Discovered in 1870, it has been worked three separate times, the last ending in 1957. In 1962 the mine tunnel became a fallout shelter, complete with food, water, and medical supplies. Pilferage, and a cave-in two years later, ended that phase of the mine's life.

BANNER

Banner is 6.7 miles east of Julian on state route 78.

Julian's one-time neighbor, Banner, is one of those "place-where" spots now. Founded in August 1870 by Julian's Louis B. Redman (who was looking for wild grapes and found gold instead), Banner was so named because, in the cant of the times, a "ban-

ner" was a prospect that looked very promising. That's one story. Another says that Redman marked his claim with a banner—a small American flag. In under a year, the town of Banner was a full-fledged competitor to Julian, featuring a two-story hotel, two stores, three saloons, and other establishments. The town, built in a narrow canyon, was washed out by floods in 1874, 1916, and 1926. It was not rebuilt after 1926, and a fire in the 1930s took what remained. A picnic area and store occupy part of the former townsite.

Several mines are hidden in the brushy hills between Julian and Banner, many along the old Banner Grade. They include some of the principal producers in the area: the Warlock (see previous entry) the Ready Relief, the Gold Cross, and many others.

The drive from Julian to Banner is still worthwhile, first because of the road: the new Banner Grade is a twisting, seven-mile creature that takes you from Julian, at an elevation of 4,220 feet, down Banner Canyon through a series of switchbacks to

Cabin at Banner

the site of Banner, at 2,755 feet above sea level. Second, there is at least one remnant worth examining. At the last switchback just before you come to Banner, a road, blocked by a locked gate, heads south. When I was there, no "no trespassing" signs were posted and there was ample evidence that people had circumvented the fence near a stream and walked in. Beyond the gate was the entrance to the old Banner Grade, and not far from the gate, across a stream, the mill of either the Ready Relief or the Redman mine (the latter spelled "Redmond" on the topographic map). It was posted against trespassing, however, so I photographed from a distance. On my side of the stream was a cabin that showed evidence of recent habitation, although it was deserted at that time.

STONEWALL MINE

The Stonewall Mine is 12 miles southeast of Julian on state route 79. As you drive from Julian, be sure to turn off at Inspiration Point overlook, which affords a stirring view down to the Banner area and beyond. When you have passed the southern end of the Cuyamaca Reservoir, signs will lead you to the mine site.

The Stonewall Mine is now part of Cuyamaca State Park, until 1933 called Rancho Cuyamaca. At one point this land played a central part in the history of the Julian-Banner Mining District. Rancho Cuyamaca was a land grant given in 1845 to Augustin Olvera; twenty-five years later, it was in the hands of four men who had purchased the property for its

timber. When gold was discovered in the Coleman City-Julian area, the four did some creative work on the boundaries of their holdings and announced that all ore found on "their land" would require a payment of royalties. The effect was a near-paralysis in mining efforts. The dispute wasn't settled in court until 1873, with the miners prevailing. But many mines that had stopped production rather than pay a royalty had fallen into disrepair and did not reopen.

The Stonewall was the result of a discovery made in 1870 by William Skidmore, who found a gold-bearing quartz vein while tracking one of his mules that had been pasturing near Cuyamaca Lake. He named the claim the Stonewall Jackson Mine, but the Jackson was dropped due to Civil War animosities.

After several owners of the mine met with very limited success, ex-Governor Robert Whitney Waterman brought the property to fruition and made it the most productive mine in San Diego County. During the years 1888–91, over $900,000 in gold was taken out, which, according to Waterman, netted "$500 in gold per day, after expenses." Operations halted in 1893 because the principal ore played out and water was filling the deeper shafts. Further attempts in 1907–08 and 1923–26 failed, culminating in the collapse of the main shaft.

At the site today sits a cabin serving as an exhibit that features outstanding historical photographs and data about the Stonewall mine. The shaft itself is surrounded by a wire fence, but easily visible inside are foundations and remnants of mining machinery and paraphernalia.

Area Three: Imperial Ghosts

HEDGES (TUMCO)

Take the Ogilby turnoff from I-8, which is 28 miles east of the last Holtville, California, turnoff, or 16 miles west of Yuma, Arizona. About 3.8 miles north of I-8 is the site of Ogilby, once the post office for the American Girl Mine and a railroad loading stop along the Southern Pacific. (Be sure to see the historic, neglected 1878 Ogilby cemetery just south of the railroad tracks on the west side of the highway at an intersection with a rural road.) Drive north 4.5 miles from the tracks and turn east where the Gold Rock Camp sign points west. (Visit the Gold Rock store, which features lots of rock-hound specialties and western memorabilia.) Hedges is .5 miles east of the highway.

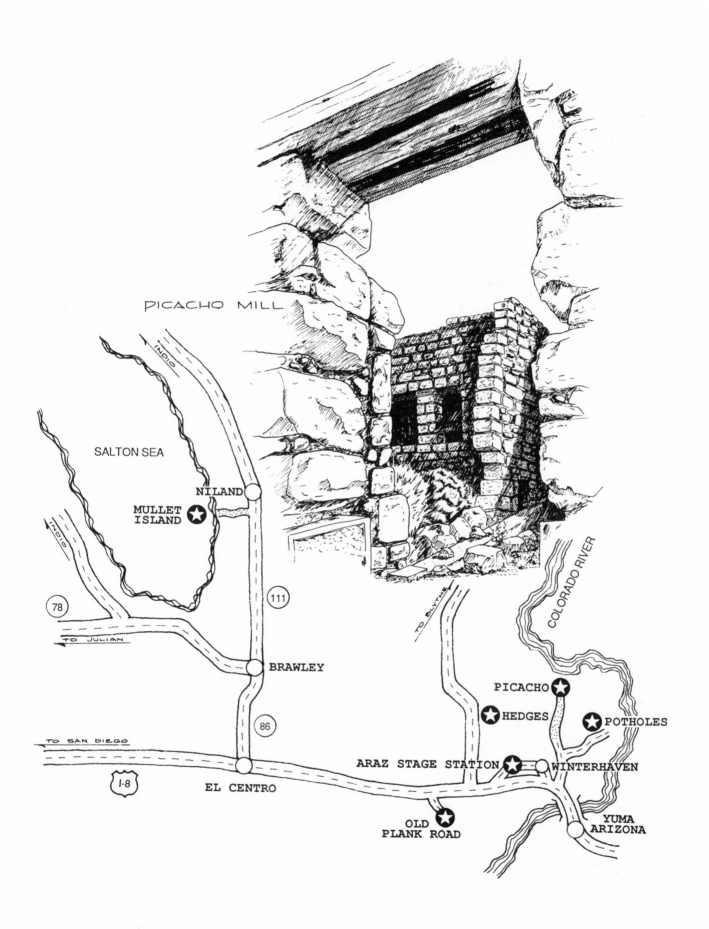

PICACHO MILL

INDIO

SALTON SEA

NILAND

MULTET ISLAND ★

INDIO

78

TO JULIAN

COLORADO RIVER

TO BLYTHE

111

BRAWLEY

86

TO SAN DIEGO

PICACHO ★

★ HEDGES

★ POTHOLES

I-8

EL CENTRO

ARAZ STAGE STATION ★ WINTERHAVEN

OLD PLANK ROAD ★

YUMA ARIZONA

Stone ruins at Hedges

On the eastern fringe of the Imperial Valley lie the Cargo Muchacho Mountains, and just in their foothills stand the sparse remains of Hedges—walls of three roofless stone buildings, extensive dumps, four cyanide vats where a large mill used to stand, and dozens of trails leading into the Cargo Muchachos. One unusual feature of Hedges is a dump-loader that was carved out of the claylike earth so that a small truck could drive up a ramp to the top of a platform and drop its load into another vehicle below. North of the site is the Hedges cemetery, in an area remarkably devoid of vegetation. There you will find, more or less enclosed by a broken-down, barbed-wire fence, more than a dozen graves covered with rocks and one comparatively elaborate concrete vault.

I feel the conflict between objective reporting and personal reaction at a ghost town like this one; the description of the site so far is, admittedly, a bit unimpressive. But I must add that I have enjoyed my visits to Hedges enormously. Perhaps it is the Desert Rat surfacing in me—the infatuation with the remote, the stark, the abandoned, that calls to so many of us Westerners. Hedges is also, I suppose, a site for the purist. I can't honestly recommend that you drive hundreds of miles to visit this site, yet I did—and felt well rewarded.

The original ore deposit was discovered on Janu-

The Tumco Mine's cyanide vats, with Cargo Muchacho Mountains behind

Piled stones form most of the graves at the Hedges cemetery.

ary 6, 1884, by Ogilby's Peter Walters, a Southern Pacific section hand. The camp that developed was initially called Gold Rock Camp. By the 1890s the camp was a company town called Hedges, named for C. L. Hedges, a vice-president of the Golden Cross Milling and Mining Company. The town of Hedges had a population of as many as 3,000 at the turn of the century and a mill of 140 stamps. For a look at the town during its boom period, consult Miller's *Ghost Towns of California,* which shows a panoramic photo of Hedges in 1905. Because it was a company town, Hedges proper was a fairly law-abiding place. Adjacent to the town, however, was—if you will—Hedges improper, which featured entertainments like the Stingaree Saloon. One humorous footnote is that Billy Horan was constable of Hedges, but he also owned the Stingaree—just out of the company's, but probably not his own, jurisdiction.

In 1910 the Golden Cross Company went into bankruptcy, and the town's name was changed to Tumco, an acronym in honor of the new owner, The United Mines Company (a subsidiary of the Borden Company). Tumco lasted only about three years and was then abandoned. The mines were worked sporadically and mostly unprofitably until 1941.

My principal problem is not whether to recommend the site—I do—it's what to call the place. Is the town Gold Rock Camp, by which it was originally known? Or is it Hedges, a name it held for about twenty years? Or is it Tumco, active for only

three years but dormant for seventy? The town is much more commonly known as Tumco among backroads people. But I let the 1963 Ogilby 15′ topographic map decide for me. The site on that map is called Hedges, with the prominent features of the townsite noted as the Hedges cemetery and the Tumco Mine. (I have since felt vindicated by that choice, since the new 7½′ map, a provisional edition of 1988, is named for Hedges.)

Incidentally, Erwin G. Gudde's *California Place*

A single concrete vault at the Hedges cemetery

Names has no entry for the Cargo Muchacho Mountains, in which Hedges nestles, and Gudde's *California Gold Camps* states that neither the origin nor the etymology of the name could be determined. But I learned of the following legend, one version of which is recorded in a Spanish, not Mexican, *cuento* (short story).

During a war with the Moors, a young Spanish boy became very ill (or severely injured, depending upon the version), and his father realized that he would have to get him to medical assistance and out of harm's way. He lifted his son across his shoulders and began a journey into the nearby mountains, on the other side of which was a settlement where he knew he could find the necessary help. Night fell as the father carried his son. He labored on all night up into a pass in the mountains and eventually down the other side of the range. He spoke to his son occasionally, and he heard his son whisper reassurance back to him.

When he arrived at the settlement, the people there relieved the man of his burden, only to discover that the boy was dead. He had been dead for hours. The replies that the father had heard had only been in his mind—or perhaps it was a miracle, for now the father was safe from the war. The mountains were named in honor of the father's heroic efforts, for Cargo [mi] Muchacho in Spanish means "I carry my boy."

PICACHO

The site of Picacho is 24 miles north of the intersection of S24 and U.S. 80, which is east of Winterhaven, California, and north of Yuma, Arizona. Follow the signs to the Picacho State Recreation Area. The Picacho Mine, currently active, comes clearly into view 4.7 miles before the townsite.

The first mining activity at Picacho probably began in 1862 when José María Mendivil discovered rich gold deposits and staked out five claims in the Picacho Basin, an area still being worked today almost five miles south of the townsite. The basin was named for nearby Picacho Peak (a Spanish-English redundancy, "Peak Peak").

David Neahr, a Yuma store owner and the builder of the Yuma Territorial Prison, became interested in the mines around Picacho because of all the gold dust that miners were bringing into his store. By 1878, Neahr had purchased several claims

and built a stamp mill along the bank of the Colorado River to process his ore. Neahr ran into financial difficulties, however, and sometime after 1880 Dr. DeWitt Jayne took over the mine and mill.

In the 1890s, the operation was sold to Stephen W. Dorsey, who, with associates, formed the California King Gold Mines Company. Dorsey had a rather checkered past—as a carpetbagger in Arkansas, as a federal bureaucrat suspected of fraud and bribery in Washington, D.C., and as a property owner in New Mexico accused in a land swindle. Dorsey erected a new mill in Picacho in 1896, capable of processing thirty times the ore of Jayne's mill, but he sold out in 1901. By 1904 Dorsey's California King Gold Mining Company was bankrupt and the site was moribund.

José María Mendivil, mentioned earlier as the probable discoverer of the gold in Picacho Basin, homesteaded a place that he called El Río, along the Colorado River. As mining activity increased, Mendivil's home became a settlement. He laid out a townsite and sold lots for the community, which became known as Picacho. At the time the mills were operating just east of the townsite, the population may have been as high as 2,500, and the payroll for the 700 men working the mines and mills was $40,000 per month. Between $13 million and $15 million in gold was transported from Picacho.

A "special contributor" to the Los Angeles *Times* reported in 1902 that Picacho was an "oasis of bustle," as a one-thousand-ton cyanide plant and a narrow-gauge railway were being constructed at the camp, but by 1910 all the mines had been closed because of a series of events. In July 1904 a main belt broke at the mill, sending a giant, twenty-one-ton flywheel sailing through the roof and landing half a mile away. Remarkably, no one was injured, but damage to the mill was extensive. Then, just over two weeks later, a torrential storm washed out the 4.5-mile Picacho and Colorado River Railroad. Next, the value of ore declined. Finally, the Laguna Dam was completed in 1909, meaning that riverboats could no longer reach Picacho from Yuma—and the damming of the Colorado River also submerged much of the town. Some mines reopened during the 1930s, but all production ceased during World War II.

The Picacho Basin certainly isn't quiet at this writing. The Picacho Mine resounds with the roar of trucks hauling ore down wide dirt roads. The area is closed to visitors, but from a turnout you can

Picacho cemetery

get a good view of the mine, with its tiny cemetery just across a small draw. Behind the mine stands dramatic Picacho Peak, with its *ventana* (window) near the top. The peak rises to an elevation of 1,947 feet, more than 1,300 feet above where you're parked. You can also see evidence of other inactive diggings in the basin as you drive toward the state recreation area.

Most visitors to Picacho take the hour's drive from Yuma to enjoy water sports and camping. Many, no doubt, never see the historic parts of the park, as they're somewhat tucked away. The townsite of Picacho is comprised of three principal attractions. The first, beyond the ranger station, is the cemetery (relocated from its original, now underwater, location), featuring several headstones—including a few of modern vintage—all enclosed inside a neat, white picket fence that seems oddly out of place in this desert setting. Picacho Peak is visible from the cemetery if you look off to the southwest.

The second and third attractions are to be found on the Picacho Mills Historic Trail and are very much worth the one-mile walk. The trail head is on the eastern end of the park on the road to the park employees' residences. Along the trail is a turnoff to the old Picacho jail—a tiny cave with bars. The average hiker will take about twenty to thirty minutes to reach the sites, but don't hurry—the desert terrain is a palette of colors, and the Colorado glides along quietly nearby. Incidentally, you might be surprised at the direction of the river. The Colorado, of course, is a north-to-south river, but here it is west-to-east. In fact, here is a geographical curiosity: When you're in Picacho, California, Arizona is to the north, east, and south.

The ruin of the upper mill, the first you'll reach, is the one that was built in 1896 by Dorsey's mining group. It features mostly foundations, retaining walls, and one large boiler. The principal reason there are so few remnants here is that the body of the mill was moved to Picacho Basin after the turn of the century. The more interesting remains are farther down the trail at the lower mill. This is the original mill, built in 1878 by David Neahr (but credited to Dr. DeWitt Jayne by a sign at the spot). The large cut-stone walls attest to the builders' confidence that the Picacho veins would be producing for many years. Plan to spend thirty to forty minutes at the millsites.

POTHOLES

Potholes is north of Yuma, Arizona, near Laguna Dam. Detailed directions are in the text.

Picacho—the ruins of Dorsey's mill, built in 1896

How much of a ghost town enthusiast are you? Do you require buildings under roof, cemeteries with verses inscribed on tombstones? Or are you willing to spend part of a morning taking wrong turns, getting dust all over the interior of your vehicle, only to arrive at a spot where exploration and investigation reveal little more than what your imagination can create? If you are the latter, then Potholes just may be for you.

Potholes was a placer-mining gold area, although adits in the vicinity testify that someone was trying for primary veins. The shallowness of the adits also attests to their lack of success. A report in the Los Angeles *Times* in 1902 claims that mining efforts at the site date from about 1720, calling Potholes "probably the oldest placer camp within the confines of the United States," but other sources put the beginnings of Potholes at around the time of the '49er Gold Rush. The townsite is riddled with sinks, holes that range from two to about ten feet deep and usually two to four feet across. These sinks, or pockets, certainly have resulted from natural geological occurrences, such as running water flooding naturally dry washes, rather than manmade mining efforts. Those deep pockets, any visitor

would decide, are the "potholes" that determined the appellation of the mining camp. *California Place Names* substantiates this, stating that the original gold deposits were found in pockets, or pots. The name became legitimized when a spur of the Southern Pacific Railroad was extended to the vicinity in 1907, during the construction of the nearby Laguna Dam, where the terminus was called Potholes.

Laguna Dam, the first built on the Colorado, was constructed of concrete, using local sand and gravel. According to author-historian Harold O. Weight, miner William G. Keiser claimed that more placer gold was contained in the materials to build the dam than the dam itself cost and that as water cascaded over the dam it etched out nuggets in the concrete. Construction workers would return after their shifts to "mine" the dam. A special passenger train from Yuma brought celebrants to the Potholes terminus on March 31, 1909, to attend the official opening ceremonies of the Laguna Dam.

At one time Potholes had a population of four to five hundred miners, most of them Mexican. The placer deposits were worked into the 1930s, with total production reported at about $2 million, al-

The cut-stone ruins of Jayne's 1879 mill, near the banks of the Colorado River at Picacho

though that seems a rather high estimate for such a small placer camp.

No major ruins, no extensive foundations, no great rubble heaps stand at Potholes. The cemetery is the most significant feature, but it is separated now from the rest of the townsite, the graves having been moved in the 1930s because of the construction of the All-American Canal. This new location is a small, parched graveyard with some sunscorched wooden markers; however, the mood of antiquity and abandonment is broken more than a little by the smooth banks of the canal nearby and the power lines almost directly overhead. One good wooden marker reads, if you inspect it carefully, "Richard Richter, died at Potholes, 1907."

At the townsite across the canal you will find the curious potholes in abundance, looking somewhat as if a crazed giant came through with an oversized post-hole digger. Be careful around this area: a few of the potholes are deep and steep enough that it would be quite difficult to get out of them. At the townsite you will see little to indicate man's presence except for broken glass and rusted tin. Beyond the main site, however, is better evidence.

Have I convinced you to give Potholes a look? Here's how you get there. Start from the intersection of U.S. 80 and rural road S24, north of Yuma, Arizona, and east of Winterhaven, California. This is the same beginning point for the route to Picacho (see previous entry). As you head north on S24, you'll come to Ross Road, where S24 turns right. The road to Pichacho proceeds straight ahead. To get to Potholes, follow S24 to the east on Ross Road. Go through the small town of Bard and then

The townsite of Potholes as viewed from the eastern bank of the All-American Canal; the potholes are to the right of the three power poles.

The sinks that gave Potholes its name

past Cole's Corner. One mile beyond Cole's Corner a sign commemorates the site of Mission San Pedro. From there a road proceeds up to the canal, but it is posted "no trespassing." The cemetery is up that road, and you should take it at your own risk. If you decide to proceed, go up to the canal and turn right, heading northeast. The cemetery is about thirty yards beyond on your right, almost beneath the power lines.

If you want to see Potholes, I recommend using a truck. Continue to Laguna Dam, which is about one mile northeast of the Mission San Pedro sign. From the dam, continue north along the paved road until the first paved road turns left, about 2.5 miles from the dam. The road is marked "closed" and

"no trespassing," although there is ample evidence that lots of people are ignoring the signs. Dozens of motor homes were camped in the desert beyond the canal when I came through. Use your own judgment. If you decide to go on, note your mileage. On the west bank of the canal, take the road to the left that parallels the water. You will shortly leave the canal and pass through a working mine area, noted on the Laguna Dam $7\frac{1}{2}'$ topographic map as the Trio Mine. You will know you are on the right road when you pass the mine headquarters about 1.5 miles from where you noted your mileage at the canal. Beyond the mine headquarters .4 mile is a turnoff to the left, which even featured a sign marking it as the turnoff to Potholes when I was there. Do not,

Potholes cemetery, near the eastern bank of the canal

however, depend upon that sign's being there. From the turnoff, take the main dirt road heading in the direction of the canal. Potholes is 1.3 miles from the turnoff (and 3.2 miles from the pavement by the canal). At the townsite you will find the distinctive potholes on your right, and you can see the canal bank beyond the site. You'll know you're at the right place because near the canal bank the power lines zig into the site down the hill from the southwest and then zag almost due north across the former mining camp.

After you have examined the main site, follow the road past the townsite and around to the left. It branches, the right going steeply up to the canal, the left heading up a sandy wash. Park here if you don't have four-wheel drive. The wash area shows evidence of mining activity and features a chimney and a foundation up to the left on a small rise. Several shallow adits are in the area. When I was there, someone was dry-panning for gold in this wash. Perhaps Potholes still pays off.

MULLET ISLAND

Mullet Island, naturally, cannot be reached by car. You can either visit it by boat or observe it from the land. To do the latter, head west on Alcott Road (the first road south of the "Y" intersection that is south of Niland) on the eastern shore of the Salton Sea. Drive 3.5 miles west on Alcott Road and park your car just beyond the intersection. Walk as far to the west as you can and observe Mullet Island through a telescope or binoculars.

The Imperial Ghosts section of this chapter is filled with what to some might be pretty minor stuff: Hedges, Picacho, Potholes. But to others they are real treasures—ignored, abandoned sites that have a beauty, a desolation, that draws the contemplative person. To that person, I suggest taking a look at Mullet Island. It's located in the Salton Sea, along an alternate route that travels between areas One and Three in this chapter. If, for example, you are planning to visit Berdoo Camp and Hedges, you could see this along the way. The joy of Mullet Island is not what is left—there is virtually nothing, merely a couple of concrete foundations. The joy is in the observing, because the island is adjacent to the Salton Sea National Wildlife Refuge, and the surroundings are absolutely of another world. Here, the water birds are the residents; you are the temporary interloper.

Mullet Island, which rises from the Salton Sea to an elevation of 190 feet below sea level, was a peninsula until the inland sea began to rise in 1948. Efforts to raise the level of the road connecting Mullet to the mainland failed. As a result, Mullet Island was formed, and the enterprises there—duck clubs, a hot-springs bathhouse, a dance hall, rental cabins, and a commercial silver-mullet fishing operation—became isolated.

A *Desert Magazine* article in July 1962 shows several buildings standing in a photograph taken in 1955; then-current photos in the same article show considerably less, although the dance hall and a few cabins remained. Now there is nothing except two walls, and—from a distance—you, and the birds.

Area Four: Lagniappe

As anyone from Bayou country can tell you, "lagniappe" is something extra, something unexpected thrown in for good measure. The last three sites in this book definitely fit into that category. They are not grouped together here because of their geographic proximity, so consult the maps in this chapter to see their locations in relation to the other sites. I am, perhaps, stretching the definition of ghost town to justify including these three sites, but I am convinced that anyone interested in the history of the West wants a few unusual, offbeat experiences, and I enjoyed these three locations thoroughly.

The reconstructed Vallecito stage station

Ruins of the Araz stage station

VALLECITO STAGE STATION

To reach the Vallecito stage station, drive 4.9 miles northeast of Banner on state route 78 to the junction of county road S2 at a spot known as Scissors Crossing (looking at a map will show you why). The stage station is 19 miles southeast of that intersection.

Vallecito was a natural place to recuperate on the trail between San Diego and the Colorado River, and in 1852 a stage station was built there that, five years later, became part of the short-lived San Diego and San Antonio mail line, which was followed by the more famous Butterfield stage. In 1934 a reconstruction of the station was completed, and today's visitor can get an excellent impression of the "amenities" of travel in pioneer days by walking around and through the building, the largest of the Butterfield stage stations that I have seen in California, Arizona, and New Mexico. On the east end of the present-day county park is a small cemetery with at least three graves, two of which are marked.

ARAZ STAGE STATION

The ruins of the Araz stage station are 3.5 miles west of Winterhaven, California, along old U.S. 80.

To view the antithesis of the Vallecito stage station, one can visit any number of ruins that are scattered across the Southwest. They tend to be considerably smaller than the one at Vallecito and no more than mere foundations—or less. One good example from the same era as Vallecito, and also a former Butterfield stage stop, is just west of Winterhaven, California.

I learned of the existence of this stage station

only by examining topographic maps of the Yuma area. On the Yuma West 7½' topo appeared "Old Araz Stage Depot," so I dutifully circled the location on the map, fully expecting it to be a vanished historic spot. To my surprise, I found several melting adobe walls, including one with a doorway, standing on the south side of U.S. 80, formerly the major highway across southern Arizona and California.

In a subsequent visit three years later, I was distressed to see that the wall with the doorway had collapsed. I spoke with a resident of Winterhaven who was quite bitter about the lack of preservation of this old Butterfield station, and I agree with him completely. The ruin is not even marked as a historic place, and it is rapidly deteriorating from the weather and from vandalism. A marker, a fence, and a little buttressing could do much for this disappearing piece of history.

OLD PLANK ROAD

The Old Plank Road lies about 20 miles west of Yuma, Arizona. If you are driving east on I-8, turn off at Gray's Well Road, an exit that is just east of the Gordon's Well exit. If you are coming from the east, you will need to exit at Gordon's Well and double back to Gray's Well Road. This is a frontage road that was formerly U.S. 80. Just before the road makes a turn and heads up a slight rise there is a small monument with a fence just beyond. Note: To return to the interstate, you must continue about one mile east to the next interstate entrance.

You must then proceed east; you will have to double back at the next exit if you wish to go west.

Could there be a more appropriate way to end a book on Southern California ghost towns than to salute the road builders who helped the pioneers get across the country? Amazingly, a genuine ghost road remains. During the second decade of this century, citizens of San Diego watched with envy as countless business and tourist dollars went to Los Angeles because of the east-west travel routes that led to that city. To mount a counterattack and encourage trade with their city, concerned San Diegans raised funds to extend a road to Yuma, Arizona.

Although road crews managed to negotiate mountain passes and wide riverbeds, the Imperial Sand Dunes west of Yuma posed an almost insurmountable problem: the volume of sand that could shift because of any brisk wind was enough to cover, indeed obliterate, any conventional road. The problem was solved in 1915 when wooden sections were connected for a distance of seven miles to lie across the sand instead of the crew's trying to plow through it. Construction crews were housed near a well "witched" by Newt Gray, the man in charge of the road crews, whose members were paid from between $.75 and $1.30 per day. Eventually a small settlement with gasoline, food, and desert survival supplies grew up at the site that became known, not surprisingly, as Gray's Well.

The plank road was finished in April 1915, the same month in which the Yuma Wagon and Automobile Bridge was floated into place across the Colorado River. Travelers could then shorten their route to the Pacific Ocean by 46 miles by taking the San Diego route. The original plank road was replaced a year later with a sturdier model, as traffic was much heavier than anticipated. Up to 3,000 vehicles per week were utilizing it.

The new plank road was a one-way thoroughfare of sections eight feet wide and twelve feet long, with occasional double-wide pullouts at intervals of about a thousand yards to allow for vehicles to pass one another. Of course, cars did not always meet each other next to a convenient pullout, and occasional arguments resulted when one car or another had to back up a considerable distance. When the road became covered with sand, traffic might be stopped for days until horse teams could be brought out to lift the road, shake it off, and place it down

again. Travel, naturally, was slow and cautious—the 60-mile drive between Yuma and El Centro often required twelve wary hours to complete. The speed limit on the plank road—ten miles per hour—was self-enforcing. At twelve miles per hour, the vehicle's ride was extremely uncomfortable; at twenty it was plainly perilous. Some people simply hired an experienced local driver to pilot their car.

In 1926 an asphalt-concrete road was constructed to replace the Old Plank Road. This highway eventually became U.S. 80, which in turn was replaced by I-8. The beginning of the destruction of this unique piece of automotive history began right after its discontinuance. And by World War II, when General George Patton's desert troops used parts of the road for firewood and tent platforms, the old road was little more than a memory. A couple of sections were saved for a museum in El Centro, and one length was reportedly sent to Greenfield Village in Michigan as part of a Ford exhibit in the 1930s called the "Road of all Nations."

The State of California clearly has chosen to let motorists pass by the Old Plank Road without alerting them to its existence. A sign designated the monument along old U.S. 80, but Interstate 8 has no such marker. Perhaps those who know best decided, probably correctly, that people who inhabit interstates aren't particularly interested in anything between spots A and Z. Or, the fewer people who know about the Old Plank Road, the less damage it will sustain. In the immediate vicinity of the remnants of the road, however, in the cooler months of the year, there are hundreds of all-terrain vehicles roaring over the dunes, so it isn't as if no one ever visits the place. I feel justified in telling you about this priceless historic treasure because I believe that the readers of this book, who naturally head for the uninhabited and unmarked, will delight in the old road and treat it with the utmost respect.

When you follow the directions given at the beginning of this entry, you will find yourself on a frontage road that is a kind of ghost highway itself—old U.S. 80, reduced to a side road to nowhere. A historical marker, no longer listed in the official book of landmarks, stands at the base of a section of the plank road adjacent to the site of what was Gray's Well. The fenced-off road stands behind the marker. Walk beside the heavy planks with their iron strappings up to the top of the rise and over the hill, where more sand-swept sections of the road head toward Yuma. There you will be struck by the

Sand-covered section of the Old Plank Road

desolation that even today is a palpable threat as temperatures pass a hundred degrees. Do pause for a moment and choose to ignore the nearby eighteen-wheelers crossing the country at the speed limit and then some. Look the other way, along the Old Plank Road and across the Imperial Sand Dunes, and try to imagine yourself in a Model T Ford, alone in the desert. Your respect for early travelers will soar.

Capsule Summary

MAJOR SITES

Julian, Banner, and the Stonewall Mine—from living town to forgotten mines
Eagle Mountain—complete mining-company town, now a prison

Lost Horse Mine—exceptional remnants in an impressive setting

SECONDARY SITES

Holcomb Valley—a variety of structures and remains "just up the hill" from San Bernardino
Hedges (Tumco)—abandoned site in a stark desert setting
Picacho—one cemetery and mill ruins in a state recreation area along the Colorado River
Berdoo Camp—foundations of an unusual town
Potholes—cemetery and a townsite

MINOR SITES

Vallecito Stage Station, Araz Stage Station, and the Old Plank Road—spots of historical interest

Mullet Island—a few foundations to view from a distance

ROAD CONDITIONS

Picacho and Potholes—unpaved roads that could pose problems in wet weather with flooded washes

Holcomb Valley, Berdoo Camp, Lost Horse Mine, Hedges, Mullet Island—good unpaved roads

All other sites—paved roads

TRIP SUGGESTIONS

TRIP 1: Holcomb Valley. Visiting the highlights of the Holcomb Valley will take one-half day. Round-trip mileage from San Bernardino, about 115 miles.

TRIP 1a: Add Llano or Calico to Trip 1 (see Chapter Three).

TRIP 2: Berdoo Camp and the Lost Horse Mine. These two locations can be easily combined into a one-day journey of about 400 miles out of the Los Angeles area.

TRIP 3: Combine Trips 1 and 2. All three areas could be visited with a pleasant overnight in the Big Bear Lake area.

TRIP 4: Julian, Banner, and the Stonewall Mine. You could see all these sites in a one-day trip out of San Diego or make the excursion more leisurely by staying overnight in Julian. Nearby state parks offer camping, and Julian itself has some fine accommodations. Round trip from San Diego, about 160 miles.

TRIP 5: Hedges, Picacho, Potholes, Araz Stage Station, and the Old Plank Road. Located in the southeasternmost part of California, these five desert attractions would involve about 440 miles of driving round trip from San Diego. That could be accomplished in one very long day or two relaxed ones.

TOPOGRAPHIC MAP INFORMATION FOR CHAPTER FOUR: GHOST TOWNS OF THE SOUTHLAND
(For map-reading assistance, consult Appendix A.)

Site	Topo Map Name	Size	Year	Importance*
Holcomb Valley	Big Bear City	7½'	1971 (pr[a] 1979)	2
Berdoo Camp	Lost Horse Mountain	15'	1958	2
Lost Horse Mine	Lost Horse Mountain	15'	1958	3
Eagle Mountain	Victory Pass	7½'	1987 prv[b]	3
Julian	Julian	7½'	1960	2
Banner	Julian	7½'	1960	2
Stonewall Mine	Cuyamaca Peak	7½'	1960 (pr[a] 1982)	3
Hedges (Tumco)	Hedges	7½'	1988 prv[b]	2
Picacho	Picacho	7½'	1964	2
	Picacho Peak	7½'	1965	2
Potholes	Bard	7½'	1965	2
	Laguna Dam	7½'	1955	2
Mullet Island	Niland	7½'	1956	2
Vallecito Station	Agua Caliente Springs	7½'	1959	3
Araz Station	Yuma (Arizona) West	7½'	1952	2
Old Plank Road	Grays Well	7½'	1964	2

[a]—photo revised (see Appendix A, "Distinguishing Characteristics")
[b]—provisional edition (see Appendix A, "Distinguishing Characteristics")

*1—essential to find and/or enjoy site to fullest
 2—helpful but not essential
 3—unnecessary to find and enjoy site

TRIP 6: Combine Trips 4 and 5. If you travel from the Julian area over to the sites in Trip 5 above, take county road S2 and stop at the Vallecito Stage Station. Total round-trip mileage from San Diego, approximately 475 miles. This would make a rewarding trip for a three-day weekend.

TRIP 7: Add Mullet Island to Trips 2, 4, or 5. If you are heading past the Salton Sea, you might consider following the eastern shore route and taking a look at Mullet Island through binoculars or a telescope. I would not recommend driving far out of the way for this site alone.

TRIP 8: Eagle Mountain. A visit to Eagle Mountain can be combined with Trip 2, Berdoo Camp and the Lost Horse Mine. Eagle Mountain is about an hour's drive east of Indio.

Appendix A: Reading Topographic Maps

A topographic ("TOE-puh-graphic" is preferred over "TOP-uh-graphic") map is a representation of natural and manmade features of a portion of the earth plotted to a specific scale. It shows locations and shapes of mountains, valleys, rivers, and lakes as well as principal works of man.

For the ghost town enthusiast, the topographic map (or "topo" or "quad") is a particularly valuable aid in locating towns in remote areas, determining where mines were near those towns, and noting what buildings or ruins were at the site when the maps were made. Topographic maps are more valuable than highway maps because they are so much more detailed. Nevertheless, some are more essential than others—although all are useful. In most cases the maps in this book are all you will need for outings. But be certain to check the Topographic Map Information pages for the various chapters before you go.

15-MINUTE AND 7½-MINUTE MAPS

The topo map sizes you will encounter most frequently are 15-minute and 7½-minute maps. There are 360 degrees of latitude and longitude to the earth and 60 minutes to each degree. A 15′ map covers one-fourth of a degree of latitude or longitude; sixteen 15′ maps cover one degree of latitude and one degree of longitude. A 7½′ map, which is larger in size than a 15′ map, actually covers only one-fourth the area of a 15′ map.

As a result, the 7½′ is much more detailed and usually far more helpful to the ghost town hunter. On a 15′ map, one inch represents about one mile; on a 7½′, one inch represents two thousand feet. Since the 7½′ covers such a small area, you must use several to cover a part of the state filled with ghost towns if you want maps for them all. For example, I required twenty-four maps for the towns in Chapter Three. But if you will consult the Topographic Map Information at the end of Chapter Three, you will discover that no topographic map is absolutely required since you have this book, and only ten others are recommended as helpful but not essential in enhancing your enjoyment of the sites in the chapter. In fact, no topographic map is absolutely required for finding sites, because you are using this book. That is in contrast to my books on Arizona and New Mexico (see Bibliography), for which several maps are requisite.

Generally, the 15′ maps are older. The U.S. Geological Survey has been replacing many of the 15′ maps with four 7½′ maps when new surveys are made. Nevertheless, the older maps can be quite valuable since a topographic map from, say, 1948 will show what was there decades ago, so the real adventurer can scour the area for nearly vanished roads and decaying foundations that are not apparent to the casual visitor.

DISTINGUISHING CHARACTERISTICS

The primary feature of a topographic map that is unfamiliar to the average person is the brown contour lines that extend throughout the map, showing steepness of slope. Quite simply, where the contour lines are close together the grade is steep; where they are far apart the land is fairly level. You may have had the experience when traveling a back road of following the gently curving line on the highway map only to discover that it is a dangerous, mountainous route. A topographic map clearly shows the terrain, so you should have a much clearer picture of the road ahead.

A second unfamiliar feature is the red lines that crisscross the map. They are particularly helpful in estimating distance, as each section they mark off is one square mile. Not all areas, however, have been surveyed for square-mile sections.

The final unfamiliar feature of the topographic map is the presence of numbers like "R. 40 E." and "T. 29 S." These refer to the map's location relative to the initial points of reference of California maps. California is unusual in the West in that it has three such points of reference. One covers a small area in the very northwestern part of the state and has no effect upon the sites in this book. The largest area in California is mapped from Mount Diablo, east of Walnut Creek in the Bay Area. Extending from there is the Mount Diablo Base Line (east-west) and the Mount Diablo Meridian (north-south). These survey lines are used to map an area that includes most of California and the entire state of Nevada. A smaller area, basically Southern California, is mapped from the San Bernardino Base Line and Meridian, which intersect just southwest of San Bernardino Peak, a mountain northeast of the city of San Bernardino.

All the ghost towns in Chapter One are mapped with reference to the Mount Diablo Base Line and Meridian. All the sites in Chapter Four use the San Bernardino Base Line and Meridian, and Chapters Two and Three have sites using both points of reference. Since you have explicit directions to each site, however, the different points of reference should cause you no difficulty as long was you are aware of their meaning when you are utilizing topographic maps.

The notations "R. 40 E." and "T. 29 S." indicate a place in the 40th range east of the Mount Diablo Meridian and the 29th township south of the Mount Diablo Baseline. A township range is an area six miles by six miles usually subdivided into thirty-six sections of one square mile each. Those sections are subdivided even further in map descriptions by referring to quarters of the sections by direction; hence, "the northeast quarter of the 35th section, Range 40 East, Township 29 South."

That particular description places the ghost town of Randsburg in the entire scheme of the topographic maps of the state of California. A person who knows how to read topographic maps can locate Randsburg within a couple of square miles in California, which is a significant skill to have when you are searching for the lost items on the face of the earth.

The margins of a topographic map contain useful information such as the scale, showing distances; the date the map was made; the location of the quadrangle of which this map is a part; the difference between true and magnetic north when the map was made; and very importantly, the names of the eight maps that border the map you have. The name of the map, incidentally, is chosen because of a prominent feature, either natural or manmade, on that map. Frequently the name of the map is the very ghost town for which you're looking.

Several topographic maps mentioned at the end of chapters are labeled "photorevised." This means that a map originally drawn in one year has been updated at a later date with aerial photographs because of additions or changes in interstate highways, dams, or other major projects.

Several others have been labeled "provisional," which means a map that has been published prior to a final version; it often has handwritten rather than typeset placenames on it. It is accurate, however; it is simply not the finished version. By the time you read this, many if not all of the provisional maps mentioned in this book will be in their final editions. Their names will not have changed.

AVAILABILITY

Topographic maps are available at many blueprint shops, hunters' or hikers' supply stores, and some bookstores. Those businesses will not appreciate the following suggestion, but you might consider simply examining the maps at a university library. Many universities have complete collections—including out-of-date maps that can be quite useful—for all fifty states. They also have photocopying machines in the library, and for a fraction of the cost of the maps you can copy them (U.S. Geological Survey maps are in the public domain, and photocopying them is perfectly legal). To prepare for the fieldwork of this book, I spent about fifteen dollars copying more than seventy maps instead of paying about $175 to buy them. Of those seventy-some maps, I found only fifty-seven to be useful (and some of them only marginally useful); they are included in the Topographic Map Information tables at the end of each of the four chapters.

Many maps are helpful for your purposes only for a very small portion of the map, such as for a road that cuts through a corner of the map on the way to the ghost town you're seeking. You really don't need the entire map, so just copy a portion of it. The copies do lose something compared to the original since they are not in color, but I did not find that to be detrimental while I was in the field.

While you're at the library, consult an index that shows all the topographic maps available for California and a topographic symbols sheet that details the various lines, colors, and symbols used in the maps. If you decide you want to own a number of maps, you can cut the cost by ordering from the source rather than buying them from a retail store. The address is:

> Branch of Distribution
> U.S. Geological Survey
> Box 25286, Federal Center
> Denver, CO 80225

A handy brochure that I consulted for this appendix is "Reading Topographic Maps" by Theodore D. Steger, available without charge at some U.S. Geological Survey offices.

COMPARING MAPS

A highway map is well suited to get you around California on major roads, but it is not appropriate for ghost town hunting on the back roads since it will not include minor roads or indicate the terrain that the roads must traverse. The Automobile Club of Southern California's highway map of the state, which is a very good highway map, shows the relative positions of, for example, Randsburg, Johannesburg, and Red Mountain (see entries, Chapter Three). It does not include Goler, but it does point out the vicinity of Garlock and Atolia, which most highway maps would not do. But the locations of those sites is about all you will learn.

On the other hand, the Johannesburg 7½' topographic map and its neighbor to the east, the Red Mountain 7½', tell you what you really need to know if you're going to explore the area thoroughly. From those two maps you can see the altitudes of each site, the placement of major streets and buildings, the hundreds of mine openings in the vicinity, the tailings ponds, the old railroad grade, the cemetery, an aqueduct, and the steepness of the terrain—particularly important in the areas of the mines. You can locate secondary roads, jeep trails, and radio antennas and power lines (very useful for keeping bearings on the back roads). In short, you can learn more from the maps than almost anyone could possibly need to know—along with lots of vital information. And yet, for all that, you actually don't *have* to have either of those maps to enjoy the sites of the Randsburg area; nevertheless, if you are an intrepid back-roads explorer, you'll appreciate the sites more if you have the maps (or photocopies, of course) in your vehicle.

The map on page 62 includes the same area as the topographic maps of the Randsburg area. Coupled with the directions included in the individual entries, this map is more useful than a highway map but far less detailed than the topographic maps. For the person who wishes to see more at a site than the obvious and to explore more of the area to get a feeling for what was once there, the topographic map is an irreplaceable aid.

Appendix B: Glossary of Frequently Used Mining Terms

Adit: A horizontal or nearly horizontal entrance to a mine.

Amalgam: An alloy of gold and mercury usually obtained by bringing gold-bearing minerals in contact with mercury in stamp batteries. The mercury is later expelled.

Arrastre (or Arrastra): An apparatus used to grind ore by means of a heavy stone that is dragged around in a circle, normally using mules or oxen.

Assay: To determine the value of a sample of ore, in ounces per ton, by testing using a chemical evaluation.

Bullion: Essentially solid (pure) gold or silver.

Charcoal Oven: Structure into which wood is placed and subjected to intense heat through a controlled, slow burning, which results in charcoal. Charcoal is a long-lasting, efficient wood fuel often used to power mills and smelters. If the oven is used to convert coal to coke, it's a "coke oven."

Chloride: Usually refers to ores containing chloride of silver.

Diggings: Used in this book in the broadest sense, as evidence of mining efforts, such as waste dumps, tailings, or placer workings. Technically, it refers to placer mining only.

Grubstake: An advance of money, food, or supplies to a prospector in return for a share of any discoveries.

Headframe: The vertical apparatus over a mine shaft that has cables to be lowered down the shaft for raising either ore or a cage; sometimes called a "gallows frame."

High-grading: The theft of rich ore, usually by a miner working for a larger firm that owns the mine.

Ingot: A cast bar or block of metal.

Mill: A building in which rock is crushed to extricate minerals by one of several methods. If this is done by stamps (heavy hammers or pestles), it's a stamp mill. If by iron balls, it's a ball mill. The mill is usually constructed on the side of a hill to utilize its slope—hence, a gravity-feed mill.

Mining District: An area of land described (usually for legal purposes) and designated as containing valuable minerals in paying amounts.

Pan: To look for gold by washing earth, gravel, or sand.

Placer: A waterborne deposit of sand or gravel containing heavier materials like gold that have been eroded from their original bedrock and concentrated as small particles that can be washed out.

Shaft: A vertical or nearly vertical opening into the earth for mining.

Sink: A depression in the surface of the land, usually without an outlet.

Smelter: A building or complex in which material is melted in order to separate impurities from pure metal.

Tailings: Waste or refuse left after milling is complete; sometimes used more generally, and incorrectly, to include waste dumps.

Tramway: An apparatus for moving materials such as ore, rock, or even supplies in buckets suspended from pulleys that run on a cable.

Waste Dump: Waste rock that comes out of the mine; rock that is not of sufficient value to warrant milling.

Appendix C: Pronunciation Guide

The place-names and other nouns below are the common pronunciations of people who inhabit the areas in which the words are used. Spanish words are given in their anglicized California versions.

Agua Caliente—AH-wah cahl-YEN-tay
Aguereberry—AWE-gur-berry
Amargosa—am-er-GO-suh
Araz—ah-RASS
Arrastre—ah-RASS-truh
Atolia—ah-TOLL-yuh
Ballarat—BAL-uh-rat or bal-uh-RAT
Bodie—BOE-dee
Caliente—cahl-YEN-tay
Cargo Muchacho—CAR-go moo-CHAH-choe
Cartago—car-TAY-go
Cerro Gordo—SAIR-oh GORE-doe
Crucero—crew-SAIR-oh
Cuyamaca—kwee-uh-MAH-kuh
Doble—DOE-bull
Dolomite—DOE-luh-mite
Ferge (Charles)—FER-jee

Havilah—HAVE-uh-luh
Inyo—IN-yoe
Ivanpah—EYE-vun-pah
Kearsarge—KIER-sardge
Llano—YAH-noe
Manzanar—MAN-zunn-are
Modoc—MOE-dock
Mojave—moe-HAHV-ee
Osdick—OZZ-dick
Paiute—PIE-YUTE
Picacho—pih-KAH-choe
Placer—PLASS-er
Rhyolite—RYE-uh-lite
Shoshone—shuh-SHOW-nee
Soledad—SOUL-uh-dad
Swansea—SWAN-see
Tecopa—tuh-KOE-puh
Tehachapi—teh-HATCH-uh-pee
Tejon (Fort)—tay-HONE
Tonopah—TOE-nuh-pah
Topographic—TOE-puh-graphic (preferred over TOP-uh-graphic)
Ubehebe—yew-beh-HEE-bee
Ulexite—yew-LEX-ite
Vallecito—vie-yuh-SEE-toe (preferred over val-uh-SEE-toe)
Wicht (Chris)—WICK

Appendix D: Driving and Walking in California

Survival tips are far too important to be relegated to an appendix of a ghost town book. Your local civil defense agency should have a pamphlet on the subject, and several good books have been written for the hiker and the four-wheel drive owner. The following guidelines are *not* intended to replace definitive books on survival techniques.

GENERAL SUGGESTIONS

1. Let someone know exactly where you're going and when you expect to return. Show them your destination on a map.
2. Have a good map with you.
3. Have a compass and know how to use it.
4. Have plenty of water with you, at least one gallon per person per day.
5. Carry ice in a cooler in case of snake or insect bites.
6. Have the necessary tools (see "Your Car," below).
7. Have the necessary survival gear (see "Survival Kit," below).
8. If your car breaks down and you're many miles from help, you are probably best off staying with the vehicle—especially in the desert heat. Use your signaling devices when appropriate (see "Survival Kit," below).
9. If you plan to do a good deal of back-roads driving, you should consider installing a citizens' band (CB) radio in your car or truck. CB radios are reasonably priced and can summon aid quickly in case of emergency, although their range is very limited.
10. Above all, stay calm. Don't do anything until you have logically evaluated an emergency situation.

YOU

Know your limitations. The desert or mountainside is no place to determine whether you are in good physical shape. If you require some sort of medication, be certain that there is an adequate supply in the survival kit. Wear comfortable clothing, including a hat, and shoes designed for walking; boots are best. Carry a watch, and a compass, canteen, and knife if you're walking any distance from the car. Know the temperature extremes in the area during a given time of year and have clothes in the car in anticipation of those extremes.

YOUR CAR

Make sure that your car is in excellent mechanical condition before you go anywhere on the back roads. Especially check tires, radiator hoses, battery, belts, and all fluid levels. Check that the spare tire is inflated properly. Carry a set of tools, spare belts, a good jack, at least one quart of oil, fuses, jumper cables, fire extinguisher, electrical tape, duct tape, baling wire or an equivalent, flares, a shovel, and a gas siphon. If yours is a four-wheel drive vehicle and you're going deep into the backcountry, you need to carry a lot more. Consult your manual or a book on the subject.

SURVIVAL KIT

The following, adapted from a kit recommended in a Civil Defense brochure, "Your Plan for Survival," should be in your vehicle at all times:

1. Small first-aid kit
2. Swiss Army knife
3. Waterproof matches
4. Good compass with a protected face
5. "Thunderer" whistle
6. Signaling mirror
7. Magnifying glass—for starting fires
8. Large-eyed needles and linen thread
9. Parachute silk, bright orange—for providing shelter, protecting the face in a sandstorm or snowstorm, straining water, and signaling
10. Aluminum foil
11. Water-purification tablets
12. Large orange balloons—for water storage or signaling
13. Candles
14. Razor blade
15. Pencil and notepaper—for leaving notes or marking a trail
16. Adhesive tape
17. Fishhooks—for setting snares
18. Assorted nails
19. A sharp belt knife
20. Parachute-type tow rope
21. Blankets
22. Some canned food and a can opener

All of the above items, except for the last three, fit compactly into a container about the size of an overnight case.

Remember: Have plenty of water. All of those cold cans of soft drinks will not be what you'll want or need if you get stranded.

Appendix E: Bicycling to and around Southern California Ghost Towns

I do not own a four-wheel drive vehicle. I ride bicycles at least 5,000 miles per year and have used them to explore ghost town sites throughout the West. I would have overlooked many of the outstanding features of several sites in this book had I not ventured around them by bicycle.

EXPLORING BY ROAD BIKE

I have used a road bike (touring or racing) to travel from one site to another in California, New Mexico, and Arizona. The restriction, naturally, is that one must stay on paved roads (or at least very solidly packed dirt ones). Some excellent rides in or near ghost town sites in this book include:

Chapter One: The Independence-Lone Pine area offers good riding except for the amount of traffic on U.S. 395. But a ride from Independence up to Kearsarge is a real challenge (and an incredible downhill on the return). You could also go from Lone Pine out to Swansea, Keeler, and Darwin, but be sure you have plenty of water. I would not recommend this trip in the summer.

Chapter Two: Death Valley, despite its name, makes for beautiful riding on the paved roads except for two limitations—the heat for much of the year and the traffic. Many of the paved roads have no shoulder to speak of, and the national monument is loaded with RV's with nice, wide mirrors. Nevertheless, the route from Beatty, Nevada, to Keeler, California, which crosses Death Valley, would be an experience for any seasoned rider. It features remarkable downhills into the valley and thigh-burning uphills on the way out. On the valley floor, the rides from Stovepipe Wells Village to Scotty's Castle and Furnace Creek Ranch (and beyond) can be outstanding if the motorized traffic is light. Another scenic area to ride, with considerably less traffic but lots of hills, is the road from Emigrant Junction south toward Trona. The March 1986 issue of *Bicycling* magazine has an informative article on riding through Death Valley.

Chapter Three: Most of this chapter crosses the desert, and much of that mileage is on high-speed roads, including I-15 and I-40. The best desert riding by road bike is in the Randsburg area, where traffic is relatively light. But the best place to ride—indeed, one of the better places in the lower half of California—is the Lake Isabella area. You could ride from Caliente to Havilah, Havilah to Lake Isabella, and even circumnavigate the lake.

Chapter Four: The most enjoyable road riding to ghost towns in this chapter is in the vicinity of Julian. Al-though many of the roads have a narrow shoulder or no shoulder at all, traffic is light on most of them except on holiday weekends. Another beautiful route to ride is the one that goes from Julian down to Scissors Crossing and on to the Vallecito Stage Station.

EXPLORING BY MOUNTAIN BIKE

The mountain bike (aka the All-Terrain Bike or ATB) is in its natural element looking for ghost towns. Although I ride far more miles per year on a road bike, the mountain bike is my workhorse. I can carry more camera gear, go more places, and see more of a site than I could by any other means of travel. I can lift the bike over fences, carry it through a canyon—in short, I can take it places even a jeep cannot traverse. This book is filled with sites that just beg for a mountain bike.

Chapter One: I examined Manzanar thoroughly because of the mountain bike. In fact, I never would even have seen the sewage-treatment plant ruins without it. I attempted to ride up to Cerro Gordo but did a lot of walking because of loose dirt on very steep hills. But I rode the back way down from Cerro Gordo to the Saline Valley, and that was an adventure.

Chapter Two: Death Valley is a mountain biker's paradise. You might try the road into Leadfield, but in Titus Canyon, after the townsite, the route gets sandy and it's a one-way road. Chloride City and Skidoo are glorious places to ride; the views are spectacular and each features several trails to follow. But the best of all is Panamint City. The steep, rocky trail cannot be ridden much of the way uphill (and I didn't have to, thanks to a welcome hitchhike from cyclists with a four-wheel drive van—see Acknowledgments), but the downhill is incredible. It is fast, jolting, and exhilarating—and dangerous. Use extreme care.

Chapter Three: I used a bicycle less in this chapter than in the other three. Nevertheless, some good riding can be found around Ragtown, Providence, Ivanpah, and the Randsburg area. Llano features good desert riding, although it can be explored as easily by truck. My favorite area, as mentioned in the road bike section, is the Lake Isabella area. The best ride I took there was by mountain bike around Keyesville.

Chapter Four: Although I drove the Holcomb Valley loop, I was itching to ride it, as the scenery is magnificent. Julian offers excellent riding for any kind of bike. The Old Banner Grade down to the Warlock Mine would be a great ride. I walked it in deep snow, but by the time you read this, I will have ridden it. Potholes makes for good desert riding, although some areas are sandy and others are rather steep. Hedges is a wonderful site to explore and is one of my favorite short mountain bike rides, with lots of trails and canyons to negotiate.

Appendix F: Sites Visited but Not Included

One important consideration in a ghost town book is the way that determinations were made about which sites to include. The reader might well ask if a site he or she has heard of or read about was ignored because I did not know of the site or if I saw it but chose not to include it. Below is a list, by chapters, of sites that I did visit but decided not to include as entries in *Southern California's Best Ghost Towns*. Each of the sites listed has, nevertheless, been an entry in at least one other ghost town book. Two basic factors have caused me not to include a site: it is either far too populated to be considered even remotely to be a ghost town (like Mojave, which is in one ghost town book but has all the fast-food restaurants California can offer), or it has too little left to be of significant value to most ghost town enthusiasts (such as Lanfair—east of Barstow—which consists primarily of a concrete slab).

Chapter One: Cartago, Lone Pine City, Owens Lake, Owenyo

Chapter Two: Confidence Mill, Tecopa, Zabriskie Station

Chapter Three: Barnwell, Bodfish, Cantil, Coolgardie, Daggett, Essex, Fenner, Goffs, Goldstone, Hart, Isabella, Lanfair, Mojave, Mountain Pass, Renoville, Riggs, Rosamond, Valjean, Vanderbilt, Vontrigger, White River

Chapter Four: Acton, Bagdad, Coleman City, Dale (Old Dale, New Dale, Dale III), Ogilby, Oro Grande (aka Orogrande and Halleck), Pushawalla, Twentynine Palms, Victorville

Bibliography

Arizona Daily Star, 4 April 1982; 20 February 1983; 25 February 1983.

Bissell, Charles A., ed. comp. *History and First Annual Report (for period ending June 30, 1938) of the Metropolitan Water District of Southern California.* Los Angeles: 1939.

Boyd, William Harland. *A California Middle Border.* Richardson, Tex.: Havilah Press, 1972.

Boyd, William Harland. *Land of Havilah.* Bakersfield: Kern County Historical Society, 1952.

Broman, Mickey. *California Ghost Town Trails.* Anaheim: Main Street Press, 1978.

Bugliosi, Vincent, with Gentry Curtis. *Helter Skelter.* New York: W. W. Norton and Co., 1974.

Burmeister, Eugene. *Early Days in Kern.* Bakersfield: Cardon House, 1963.

California Geology, April 1983: 75–82.

California Historical Landmarks. Sacramento: Department of Parks and Recreation, State of California, 1981.

Carter, William. *Ghost Towns of the West.* Menlo Park, Calif: Lane Publishing Company, 1978.

Chalfant, W. A. *Death Valley: The Facts.* Stanford, Calif.: Stanford University Press, 1930.

Chalfant, W. A. *The Story of Inyo.* Chicago: Hammond Press, 1922.

Clark, Lew, and Ginny Clark. *High Mountains and Deep Valleys: The Gold Bonanza Days.* San Luis Obispo, Calif.: Western Trails Publications, 1978.

Colorado River Aqueduct News, 25 October 1939.

Death Valley: A Guide. Federal Writers' Project of the Works Progress Administration. Boston: Houghton Mifflin, 1939.

Desert Magazine, June, 1958; December, 1958; April, 1961; May, 1961; June, 1961; September, 1961; July, 1962; February, 1963; May, 1963; May, 1964.

Ellsberg, Helen. *Mines of Julian.* Glendale, Calif.: La Siesta Press, 1972.

Florin, Lambert. *California Ghost Towns.* Seattle: Superior Publishing Co., 1971.

Gudde, Erwin G. *California Gold Camps.* Berkeley: University of California Press, 1975.

Gudde, Erwin G. *California Place Names.* Berkeley: University of California Press, 1949.

Hensher, Alan, and Jack Peskin. *Ghost Towns of the Kern and Eastern Sierra: A Concise Guide.* Los Angeles: private printing, 1980.

Hensher, Alan, and Vredenburgh, Larry. *Ghost Towns of the Upper Mojave Desert.* 3d ed. Los Angeles: private printing, 1987.

Hubbard, Paul B. *Ballarat: Panamint Valley Ghost Town.* Death Valley '49ers and Eastern California Museum Association, 1963.

Hubbard, Paul B.; Doris Bray; George Pipkin. *Ballarat: Facts and Folklore.* Lancaster, Calif.: private printing, 1965.

Inyo Register, 27 June 1986.

Johnson, Hank. *Death Valley Scotty: The Fastest Con in the West.* Corona del Mar, Calif.: Trans-Anglo Books, 1974.

Johnson, Robert Neil. *California-Nevada Ghost Town Atlas.* Susanville, Calif.: Cy Johnson and Son, 1967.

Keeling, Patricia Jernigan, ed. *Once Upon a Desert.* Barstow, Calif.: Mojave River Valley Museum Association, 1976.

Kirk, Ruth. *Exploring Death Valley.* Stanford, Calif.: Stanford University Press, 1956.

Leadabrand, Russ. *Desert Country.* Exploring California Byways, vol. 3. Los Angeles: Ward Ritchie Press, 1969.

Leadabrand, Russ. *Guidebook to the Mojave Desert of California.* Los Angeles: Ward Ritchie Press, 1966.

Likes, Robert C. and Glenn R. Day. *From This Mountain: Cerro Gordo.* Bishop, Calif.: Chalfant Press, 1975.

Lingenfelter, Richard. *Death Valley and the Amargosa: A Land of Illusion.* Berkeley and Los Angeles: University of California Press, 1986.

Los Angeles Times, 8 June 1902.

Love, Frank. *A Guide to Ghost Towns and Mining Camps of the Yuma and Lower Colorado Region.* Colorado Springs, Colo.: Little London Press, 1980.

Metropolitan Water District. *Colorado River Aqueduct.* 1st, 3rd, and 4th eds. Los Angeles: March 1935, March 1937, March 1939.

Michaelis, Bob. "Splinters Off the Plank Road." *Westerners International* (Fall 1983): 3, 4. First published in *Buckskin Bulletin.*

Miller, Donald C. *Ghost Towns of California.* Boulder, Colo.: Pruett Publishing Co., 1978.

Miller, Ronald Dean. *Mines of the High Desert.* Glendale, Calif.: La Siesta Press, 1968.

Murbarger, Nell. *Ghosts of the Glory Trail.* Los Angeles: Westernlore Press, 1956.

Murphy, Robert J. *Wildrose Charcoal Kilns.* Bishop, Calif.: Chalfant Press, 1972.

Myrick, David F. *The Northern Roads.* Railroads of Nevada and Eastern California, Vol. 1. Berkeley: Howell-North Books, 1962.

Myrick, David F. *The Southern Roads.* Railroads of Arizona, Vol. 1. Berkeley: Howell-North Books. 1975.

Myrick, David F. *The Southern Roads.* Railroads of Nevada and Eastern California, Vol. 2. Berkeley: Howell-North Books, 1963.

Nadeau, Remi. *Ghost Towns and Mining Camps of California.* Los Angeles: Ward Ritchie Press, 1965.

Nevadan, 26 December 1982.

Old Harmony Borax Works. San Bernardino: Inland Printing and Engraving Co., 1962. (Prepared from records of United States Borax and Chemical Corporation).

Paher, Stanley W. *Colorado River Ghost Towns*. Las Vegas: Nevada Publications, 1976.

Paher, Stanley W. *Death Valley Ghost Towns*. Las Vegas: Nevada Publications, 1973.

Pipkin, George C. *Pete Aguereberry: Death Valley Prospector and Gold Miner*. Trona, Calif.: Murchison Publications, 1982.

Robinson, W. W. *The Story of Kern County*. Los Angeles: Title Insurance and Trust Co., 1961.

Smith, Genny Schumacher, ed. *Deepest Valley*. Los Altos, Calif.: William Kaufmann Inc., 1978.

Starry, Roberta Martin. *Exploring the Ghost Town Desert*. Los Angeles: Ward Ritchie Press, 1973.

Sunset Magazine (March 1988, October 1988).

True West Magazine (January–February 1979).

Varney, Philip. *Arizona's Best Ghost Towns*. Flagstaff, Ariz.: Northland Press, 1979.

Varney, Philip. *New Mexico's Best Ghost Towns*. Albuquerque: University of New Mexico Press, 1987.

Weight, Harold O. *Lost Mines of Old Arizona*. Twenty-nine Palms, Calif.: The Calico Press, 1959.

Weis, Norman. *Helldorados, Ghosts and Camps of the Old Southwest*. Caldwell, Idaho: Caxton Printers, 1977.

Wolle, Muriel Sibell. *The Bonanza Trail*. Chicago: Swallow Press, 1953.

Wynn, Marcia Rittenhouse. *Desert Bonanza: The Story of Early Randsburg*. Glendale, Calif.: Arthur H. Clark Co., 1963.

MISCELLANEOUS BROCHURES

Ackerman, G. Frank. "A Walking Tour of Death Valley Ranch." Bishop, Calif.: Chalfant Press, 1981.

[State of] California, Department of Parks and Recreation. "Picacho State Recreation Area," n.d.

National Park Service. "Death Valley," "Joshua Tree," n.d.

"Randsburg Desert Museum," n.d.

Index

Note: "m" after page number indicates map; "p" indicates photo; "t" indicates topographic map information.